SPIES

SPIES

Treachery, Secrecy, Paranoia

PAULA SCHMITT

CURIOUS READS

An imprint of URTEXT
Unit 6 53 Beacon Road
London SE13 6ED

Printed and bound in Great Britain by TJ International

ISBN 978-1-912475-03-2

CONTENTS

INTRODUCTION

THE ASSASSINATION THAT WASN'T

On the morning of 25 September 1997, Khaled Meshaal, the head of the political bureau of the Palestinian resistance group Hamas, was walking to his office in Amman, the Jordanian capital where he was living in exile. Unbeknownst to Meshaal, two Mossad agents disguised as tourists were waiting for him. One was holding a can of soda; the other was concealing a syringe filled with a poison that would kill the Palestinian without leaving a traceable cause of death.

As Meshaal arrived, the assassins walked by and sprayed the poison on his neck, but Meshaal thought nothing of it. Even though he did feel something cold and wet on his skin, he also saw one of the men opening the can of soda right at that moment, and his brain did exactly what it was supposed to do: it filled the logical gap of the unexplained wet sensation with the elucidating fizzy drink.

The order for the murder had come from Benjamin Netanyahu, Israel's Prime Minister. It was supposed to be a quiet assassination, a clandestine hit that would make it look like Meshaal had died of natural causes. Mossad had been testing the plot for months on unsuspecting people in the streets of Tel Aviv, using water instead of poison, and Netanyahu was satisfied with the rehearsals. But in real life, while Meshaal reacted like he was supposed to do, his bodyguard, Muhammad Abu Saif, did not. He grew suspicious as the two agents sprinted away, and followed them in his car as they headed for refuge in the Israeli embassy. Abu Saif knew how to navigate the streets of Amman better than the assassins and soon caught up with them. He tackled the men, and a passer-by helped him take the Israelis to prison. Meanwhile, on the other side of town, Meshaal became ill, was taken to the hospital, and soon fell into a coma.

For Israel, the failed plot risked becoming a diplomatic disaster. With the spies in prison, the world would soon learn of the assassination attempt, and King Hussein of Jordan would feel betrayed by his allies conducting a clandestine operation in a country with which they had a peace agreement. Worse yet, the operation targeted a man Hussein had vowed to protect. Even if the King had been secretly informed of the plot, as some have since suspected, he now had to save face and make Israel pay for the crime, dissipating any suspicion of collusion between him and the Zionist state.

At first, the Jordanian government denied to journalists that there had been an assassination attempt on a member of Hamas. Privately, however, King Hussein demanded that Israeli officials immediately send the antidote to the poison that was shutting down Meshaal's respiratory system. Netanyahu initially refused. Danny Yatom, the head of Mossad, flew by helicopter to try to contain the situation in Amman but didn't bring the antidote with him. He later recounted that on that day he prayed twice: first for the death of Meshaal, and the second time for his recovery.

Netanyahu finally agreed to send the antidote, only after US President Bill Clinton interceded. As restitution for the Israeli betrayal, Hussein demanded and attained the release of dozens of Palestinians and members of Hamas jailed in Israel, including the leader Ahmad Yassin, the wheelchair-bound founder of the resistance group who was on the eighth year of a life sentence. Danny Yatom was replaced as head of Mossad the following year.

CHAPTER ONE

MOSSAD AND AMAN

"By way of deception, thou shalt do war." This used to be the motto of Mossad, the main Israeli intelligence agency. As far as espionage goes, it doesn't get more candid than that. Taken from the Old Testament, this inside slogan was revealed in *By Way of Deception*, a groundbreaking book by Victor Ostrovsky about his time as a Mossad agent, or *katsa*. But if the motto has since been abandoned, the mission hasn't.

Mossad is so secretive that until recently the name of its chief was kept hidden until his term was over, and its budget still remains entirely classified. But the agency has filled the blank spaces with an image carefully constructed through tailor-made news and movies, associating itself with the *007* lore that gives a heroic veneer to spy missions, while disowning operations that reminisce of the weak and cowardly. Espionage agencies generally live on fame from the former, but much of their work is based on the latter.

Renowned for the targeted assassinations carried out by its Kidon squad, Mossad is virtually unknown for its Department of Psychological Warfare, or *Loh Ammah Psichologit*, which conducts the less photogenic missions at which the agency excels. One of LAP's earliest operations was blackmailing Egyptian soldiers in the run-up to the 1967 war. To that end, family and friends of servicemen were called or sent letters with true, or even false, news of the soldiers' alleged homosexuality, as well as other potentially embarrassing or damaging information. The fear of having those rumours spread primed the soldiers for extortion. For those who wouldn't succumb to blackmail, death was the preferred choice. In his 800-page tome on Mossad, *Gideon's Spies*, Gordon Thomas describes how "a teacher at school was called by a sympathetic-sounding woman to be told that the only reason a pupil was doing badly was because her father, a senior [Egyptian] officer, had a secret male lover." After that call, the man shot himself.

Mossad never formally refuted Thomas's book, nor did it sue him for its revelations. Thomas interviewed several former officers, including Rafi Eitan, the intelligence officer who directed the capture of Nazi fugitive Adolf Eichmann, and Mossad and Aman official-gone-rogue Ari Ben Menashe. Former Mossad Chief Meir Amit was also interviewed and allegedly provided the book with a blurb: "Tells it like it was—and like it is." Considering that he was responsible for the disgraceful episode described above, one can only imagine what must have been left out.

One of Mossad's most notorious failures is the Lillehammer Affair. After the 1972 Munich Olympics attack that ended with the death of eleven Israeli athletes, assassins from Kidon started to hunt down suspects, killing them one by one using methods as formidable as poisoned chocolate, a hit-and-run car accident, and an exploding telephone. But one of those targets turned out to be an innocent Algerian waiter in Norway, whom the Mossad allegedly confused with Ali Hassan Salameh, the head of the Palestinian group Black September. This case, so notorious it has earned its own encyclopedia entry, can probably be filed under the failures Mossad didn't mind exposing, for it is a small drop of error that only serves to accentuate its ocean of incredibly successful hits. Other failures—as well as triumphs—have never been admitted, and won't be until irrefutable proof is unearthed.

The Lavon Affair perfectly illustrates that denial is the first line of defence for spy agencies, and that it can take very long for it to collapse. In 1954, a series of bombs exploded throughout Egypt. On 2 July, the post office in Alexandria was destroyed, and about two weeks later a movie theatre owned by a British company was struck, as was a US diplomatic office. The explosions looked like the work of the Muslim Brotherhood, or perhaps the action of some revolutionary group, but it was planned and executed by the Directorate of Military Intelligence, or Aman, arguably the most powerful Israeli spy agency. It took fifty-one years for Israel to admit that the Lavon Affair had been its own operation.

For the tax-paying public, the ultimate justification for a ruthless government agency that works in the shadows

For the tax-paying public, the ultimate justification for a ruthless government agency that works in the shadows is the initial problem it purports to solve, a fire fought with more fire.

is the initial problem it purports to solve, a fire fought with more fire. But in the world of espionage, it is difficult to know who started the fire first. In 1946, agents of the Zionist paramilitary group Irgun disguised themselves as Palestinian workers and set bombs in the King David hotel in Jerusalem, killing ninety-one people, among them seventeen Jews. From Paris, David Ben Gurion, one of the founders of the State of Israel, called the perpetrators "enemies of the Jews." His opinion, it turns out, wasn't shared by Israel's officialdom. Menachem Begin, the man who led the operation, ended up becoming Israel's Prime Minister, and Irgun was absorbed into the Israel Defence Forces. Support for that attack can be witnessed even today at its anniversary commemoration, graced by the likes of Benjamin Netanyahu praising the "freedom-fighters" that some Israelis consider terrorists.

Blaming someone else for one's crime is customary procedure in the world of intelligence. One of the most widely used stratagems is known as 'false flag', an attack that scores at least two points at once: incriminating an innocent enemy, and making the agency that committed the crime appear necessary and even more deserving of state funds and leeway. One of the most perplexing military attacks in recent history is suspected of having been a botched false flag operation.

On 8 June 1967, a US technical ship was in the Mediterranean helping Israel win the Six Day War against Arab states. Officially neutral, the US had sent the USS *Liberty* to monitor communications between Israel's enemies and the Soviets. And then, in one of the most baffling cases of friendly fire, four Israeli fighter jets went on a torpedoing rampage against the US surveillance vessel, killing thirty-four people on board and wounding 171. Israel has always claimed it was a case of mistaken identity, alleging that it thought it was bombarding an Egyptian ship. But fifty years later, declassified US documents show the virtually unanimous conviction among US officials, and more than two dozen survivors located and interviewed by the *Chicago Tribune*, that Israel had full knowledge it was attacking an American ship, and that it did so on purpose.

The USS *Liberty* was shelled with machine guns, cannons, and even napalm bombs, as its crew was lying on the deck bathing in the sun. There's an Israeli audio recording between the controller directing the attack and his superior in Tel Aviv verbally confirming the target as an American warship. At the moment, only eight people had been killed by Israel. Inexplicably, the attack not only didn't stop—it intensified. Fourteen minutes after that recorded communication, Israel attacked the vessel again, using more jets and even boats, killing another twenty-six people.

According to Steve Forslund, a US intelligence analyst at the Air Force base in Omaha monitoring communications for the highest office responsible for military strategic planning, "The [Israeli] ground control station stated that the target was American and for the aircraft to confirm it. The aircraft did confirm the identity of the target as American, by the American flag," he told the *Chicago Tribune*. "The ground control station ordered the aircraft to attack and sink the target and ensure they left no survivors." According to the *Tribune*, "Forslund said he clearly recalled the obvious frustration of the controller over the inability of the pilots to sink the target quickly and completely." More distressingly yet is the reaction from the highest US war official. Upon learning that the *Liberty* was under attack and needed help, Defence Secretary Robert McNamara "retorted that 'President [Lyndon] Johnson is not going to go to war or embarrass an American ally over a few sailors.'" In the most disquieting bit of the *Tribune* report, McNamara doesn't deny any of those charges. When asked about the events, the 91-year-old said: "I absolutely have no recollection of what I did that day," except that "I have a memory that I didn't know at the time what was going on."

No serious analyst believes Israel was planning to declare war on the USA, but there is little doubt the attack was deliberate. One possible explanation is that it was a false flag operation gone wrong, intent at blaming Egypt and making the US finally enter the war against the Arabs. Another conjecture is that Israel feared the USS *Liberty* had been monitoring its own communications, not only the Arabs', and inadvertently learned of its nascent nuclear program. Strategically, it would be less damaging to have to apologize for the wrongful but allegedly unintentional killing of friendly soldiers, than to confess to the illegal and deliberate manufacturing of nuclear weapons.

To most people, that sounds too cold and calculating to be believed. But such creative moral arithmetic is the essence of war and espionage: the death of one person weighed against that of two, or the value placed on life based on standing, race or rank.

Non-state actors, including some enemies of Israel, also use cold calculation in battle. In the 2006 war in

Lebanon, Hezbollah made use of guerrilla warfare tactics that some believe were inspired by Mao and his admonition that insurgents should live among the people "like fish in the water". By hiding many of its fighters and weapons in urban areas, Hezbollah induced Israel to kill civilians whenever it tried to attack the guerrillas. The more civilians killed by Israel, the bigger the propaganda coup for Hezbollah. Another cold logic applied by the Israeli army is known as 'Hannibal Procedure', a directive it kept secret for years which determines that a soldier must kill a fellow Israeli soldier if the latter risks being captured and eventually used in a prisoner exchange agreement.

Mossad suffers no shortage of impressively executed assassinations of its avowed enemies, often disguised in the media as begrudging confessions instead of what they really are: the bragging of Mossad's prowess. But the agency's less-than-brave callousness is almost never exposed, and it may have been behind one of the most stunning claims in Ostrovsky's book, reiterated later by Thomas Gordon. In what would become one of the most deadly attacks on American troops, on 23 October 1983, a truck with almost a ton of explosives drove at full speed and crashed into the Beirut headquarters of the US 1st Battalion 8th Marines. The attack, possibly orchestrated by the Shia militia Islamic Jihad, killed 241 people, 220 of them US marines. According to Ostrovsky and Thomas, Mossad was aware of the plan months before it happened, knowing exactly which truck was going to be used and having it under its surveillance. Although the US and Israel had an agreement about shared intelligence, Mossad refused to inform its US counterparts of the imminent

Such creative moral arithmetic is the essence of war and espionage: the death of one person weighed against that of two, or the value placed on life based on standing, race or rank.

Mossad's interference in other countries' politics goes way beyond its territorial interests. It has mediated the sale of weapons to several countries, sometimes illegally re-selling for a higher price what Israel got from the US.

attack. "We are not there to protect Americans," said Mossad chief Nahum Admoni.

It is also believed that Mossad could have prevented at least the death, if not the kidnapping and torture, of William Buckley, CIA station chief in Beirut. In an interview with Thomas, CIA director William Casey corroborates that theory: "Next thing [Mossad chief Nahum] Admoni was selling us a bill of goods that the PLO [Palestine Liberation Organization] were behind the kidnapping. We knew the Israelis were always ready to blame Yasser Arafat for anything, and our people did not buy at first. But Admoni was very plausible. He made a good case. By the time we figured it wasn't Arafat, it was long over for Buckley. What we didn't know was that Mossad had also been playing real dirty pool—supplying the Hezbollah with arms to kill the Christians while at the same time giving the Christians more guns to kill the Palestinians."

Mossad's interference in other countries' politics goes way beyond its territorial interests. It has mediated the sale of weapons to several countries, sometimes illegally re-selling for a higher price what Israel got from the US. It armed the white supremacists in South Africa and, allegedly, sold chemical weapons to Iran through the Israeli dealer Nahum Manbar, according to the stomach-churning book *The Shadow World: Inside The Global Arms Trade*, by Andrew Feinstein. As it did in Lebanon, Mossad has often armed opposing sides in the same war. In Sri Lanka, it sold the government PT boats for coastal patrol, while it supplied the Tamil Tigers with anti-PT boat equipment. According to Ostrovsky, Mossad also "helped Sri Lanka cheat the World Bank and other investors out of millions of dollars to pay for all the arms" they were buying from Israel. Along with Aman, Mossad also mediated Israeli weapon sales simultaneously to Iraq and Iran, proving the old adage that the only winner in a war is the one selling the guns.

One unlikely middleman for Mossad was Robert Maxwell, the media magnate who owned the British *Daily Mirror* and *Sunday Mirror* tabloids, and later the Israeli *Maariv*. Maxwell collaborated in many ways: mediating weapons sales, hiding millions of dollars for Mossad in secret bank accounts, and even stealing from the Mirror Group pension fund money he allegedly advanced to Mossad for a shady financial transaction. After a disagreement with his handlers in Israel, his cover was blown and the world learned he was a Mossad asset. Shortly after, his body was found in the sea.

Maxwell had also helped Mossad catch Mordechai Vanunu, the man that revealed Israel's nuclear weapons factory in Dimona who was eventually deceived by a female *katsa* and snatched in Italy. Maxwell used his newspaper to try and destroy Vanunu's reputation, but the man's character was hard to tarnish. Vanunu never demanded a penny for his sacrifice, and refused all Nobel Peace Prize nominations, asking the committee that his name be taken off the list that once honoured the very man credited with having started Israel's nuclear program, Shimon Peres. He spent eighteen years in prison, most of them in solitary confinement, and now lives as a prisoner of conscience, forbidden from leaving Israel or talking to foreign journalists. According to Seymour Hersh in the meticulously researched *Samson Option*, Peres personally supervised the capture of Vanunu because he feared the whistle-blower would reveal the fact—virtually ignored by the mainstream media—that Israel "deployed nuclear land mines along the Golan Heights" on the border with Syria.

Mossad's motivations for certain types of foreign meddling are baffling, and are often dismissed outright as conspiracy theories for lacking any obvious connection to territorial interests, or not providing Israel with immediate, quantifiable profit. One of the most intriguing of those cases is told in *Gideon's Spies*, an allegation later repeated by other authors. According to Thomas, Henri Paul, the man who drove the car in which he died along with Princess Diana and Dodi Al Fayed, was in Mossad's payroll. Paul, the head of security of the Ritz Hotel in Paris, was allegedly blackmailed into collaborating after Mossad threatened to reveal he was selling information about celebrities to the paparazzi. Mossad is also widely understood to have bugged Monica Lewinsky's house phone while she carried out an affair with President Bill Clinton, just as Israel hoped for the pardon of its spy Jonathan Pollard, convicted of selling it US military top secret information. As a curious side note, the movie *Wag the Dog* anticipates by months an image that would become an iconic scene of the Clinton-Lewinsky scandal: in the dark comedy about a US president who fabricates a war to divert attention from his sexual misconduct, TV screens show the president greeting his beret-wearing school-age lover, uncannily resembling a reality that no one yet knew was real.

In espionage, covert operations conceal the identities of their perpetrators, while clandestine operations are

Mossad's clandestine operations are facilitated by an unusual advantage it has over other agencies: its extensive network of collaborators known collectively as sayanim. *A sayan is a Zionist who will work and live a normal life until called to help with providing some sort of cover.*

themselves concealed and kept so secret they are not suspected of having even happened. In the summer of 1980, Mossad conducted a covert operation to get rid of a scientist, and a clandestine operation to get rid of the prostitute it had hired to distract the victim. According to Ostrovsky, two agents in Paris slit the throat of Yahya El Mashad, the Egyptian physicist heading Iraq's nuclear program, after he refused to collaborate with Israel. Marie Express, the prostitute hired by the agents to be with Mashad the night before, realized her clients may have had something to do with the death. Scared, she went to the police, and later confided information to a man who then passed it on to Mossad. One night, as Marie worked the Boulevard St-Germain, "a man in a black Mercedes pulled up to the curb and motioned her to come around the driver's side," when another black Mercedes "proceeded at high speed down the avenue. Just at the right moment, the driver in the parked car gave [Marie] a heavy shove, sending her flying backward into the path of the oncoming car" and killing her instantly.

Mossad's clandestine operations are facilitated by an unusual advantage it has over other agencies: its extensive network of collaborators known collectively as *sayanim*. A *sayan* is a Zionist who will work and live a normal life until called to help with providing some sort of cover (a workplace, a telephone number, a hideout, a rental car, a bank account, etc.). Most sayanim will help Mossad for free. According to Ostrovsky, in London alone there were around two thousand sayanim in 1990.

Sayanim, or maybe full-blown agents, were used in one of the most inexplicable concurrences known to have happened on American soil. After a four-month-long investigation, Christopher Ketcham of *Salon.com* revealed that "for almost two years, hundreds of young Israelis falsely claiming to be art students haunted federal offices—in particular, the DEA [Drug Enforcement Administration]." According to Ketcham, "Reports of the mysterious Israelis with an inexplicable interest in peddling art to G-men came in from more than forty U.S. cities and continued throughout the first six months of 2001. [...] Agents of the DEA, ATF [the Bureau of Alcohol, Tobacco, Firearms and Explosive], Air Force, Secret Service, FBI, and US Marshals Service documented some 130 separate incidents of 'art student' encounters. Some of the Israelis were observed diagramming the inside of federal buildings. Some were found carrying photographs they had taken of federal agents," and visiting offices that were not known by the public and didn't have a street address. They also "visited the homes of numerous DEA officers and other senior federal officials." More puzzling yet, not a single one of those self-proclaimed students was enrolled in an art school. One of them was found in possession of bank receipts amounting to withdrawals of almost US$180,000. It is perplexing that such a story—as fully documented as it is—was overlooked by almost every other news outlet.

One type of clandestine mission seamlessly performed by Mossad is the destruction of its enemies' reputation through allies in the mainstream media. Some of these allies are sayanim providing services for ideological reasons; others are blackmailed into doing so, while others still just do it for the money. All of them have been crucial in helping Mossad's LAP department spin stories blaming

Palestinians or Muslims for things like the TWA accidental explosion, or the bombing at the Atlanta Olympic Games. The purview of Mossad is obscure and it can go far and wide. Ostrovsky says the agency used to counterfeit Jordanian dinars to not only save their own money, but to also flood the neighbouring country with currency and cause inflation. Yet with all those disparate undertakings, when it comes to actually countering terrorism, Mossad can appear disconcertingly carefree.

In September 2013, I attended the four-day terrorfest known as the World Summit on Counter-Terrorism in Herzliya, Israel, with the confirmed presence of several high officials in Israeli, US, and UK intelligence, including former heads of Mossad and Aman, and the Israeli Minister of Defence. With so many terror fighters all gathered in one place, and all of them so aware of the threat of terror, one would think there would be an unprecedented level of security. But then one would be quite wrong. There was not even a functioning metal detector. Nametags were not verified, and bags were not searched. Personally, I was almost insulted with the ease with which my application was accepted—they clearly hadn't read my fictional book about a journalist vigilante who wants to assassinate some of the scoundrels she interviews.

There was one thing, however, that seemed to have scared those fearless officials: the screening of the documentary *The Gatekeepers*. Announced and printed in the official program, the documentary was inexplicably cancelled, along with a panel discussion with its director, Dror Moreh. I wasn't surprised with the cancellation; I had been surprised that counterterrorists would show a documentary in which Yuval Diskin, former head of the Israeli police Shin Bet, says the following words:

> "To put it cynically, luckily for us, terrorism increased. Why do I say that? Because now we had work and we stopped dealing with the Palestinian state."

I had that line memorized, and decided to ask former Mossad chief Shabtai Shavit about that proposition, but he refused to talk to me. I tried again, and again he said no. Undeterred, I went to his lecture and sat beside his wife, a lovely and elegant woman who sympathetically heard how much I was interested in counterterrorism. After the lecture, she introduced me to her husband and convinced him to speak to me. Shavit and I met in an empty conference room. He never allowed me to record the conversation, but let me type it on my computer. The interview would eventually be published in the Israeli *972mag.com*, the only outlet that accepted my story. In it, as I built up to the theory I wanted to explore, Shavit admitted that propaganda was very important for Israel. Indeed, he said PR is "one of the pillars of our existence." In light of that admission, I asked him whether Israel's image improved every time there was a suicide attack against Israelis. He then abruptly interrupted my question and held my arm: "I think you're going down a slippery slope now. Let's stop this," he said, and then asked me, "How long are you staying here?" Puzzled by the sudden curiosity, I asked whether he was thinking of assassinating me, to which Shavit replied with a smile and a very strong Hebrew accent: "I have never assassinated a beautiful lady."

Mossad's proficiency at assassination is so legendary that it has created its own franchise. It trains several police forces around the world, and it has been hired for outsourced killings that other foreign intelligence outfits cannot, or will not, conduct themselves. Openly working with Britain and the US, Mossad has collaborated less publicly with the Pakistani intelligence agency ISI, Saudi Arabia, the United Arab Emirates, and Bahrain. According to Yossi Melman, co-author of the best-selling book on Israeli intelligence *Every Spy a Prince*, once they leave their outfits, veterans of Mossad and the Israeli armed forces often end up working as "consultants, trainers for the most brutal regimes in the world, training drug dealers in Colombia, assisting dictators in Africa, working with brutal regimes in Central America."

CHAPTER TWO

ON THE COUCH

Spies frequently make psychological profiles of people, but what is the profile of a spy? What are the personality traits common to those whose work entails secrecy, dishonesty, risk, betrayal, and the self-obliteration required by a necessary double life?

By their own admission, spies are essentially traitors—either to their country, if they are double agents, or to the trusting individuals they interact with and deceive. They live a type of moral duplicity according to David Charney, a psychiatrist who has woxarked for the intelligence community for decades and was assigned by the CIA to do psychiatric evaluations. "When they go overseas," Charney says, "their job is to lie and steal, and they are okay with that because they see it as being part of their patriotism toward their country."

While intelligence-gathering may be legal, espionage

is not, and countries that do not have the death penalty may even create an exception for people caught spying for a foreign power. But is patriotism the main motivation for a spy? Is there indeed some selfless purpose driving those who make friends in order to deceive them? And what about the risks faced by an agent? Are they merely tolerated because of this higher purpose, or are they incentives instead? Are these people courageous or spineless? Immoral or selfless?

Experts on the subject and members of the intelligence community cite four main reasons why people become spies: money, ideology, coercion and ego. MICE, the resulting self-explanatory acronym, was initially used to define the motivations for a traitor, but it has long become widely accepted for spies in general. While money is a natural motivation for spies—much like it is for any salaried employee in other fields—for double agents and traitors *more* money is a good reason for deceit. Randy Burkett, CIA representative at the US Naval Postgraduate School, noted that, "In a study of 104 Americans who spied [for enemy countries] and were caught between 1947 and 1989, the majority, indeed an increasing number over the years, reported that money was their sole or primary motivator."

But, whereas money is a primary motivator, moral narratives are crucial for efficient recruiting, while enemies are crucial for moral narratives. Without a foreign enemy, the killing and stealing would lack any redeeming qualities. Governments justify the moral trespass of secret service procedures based on perceived threats to the nation, which also help satisfy two other MICE criteria: Ideology and

Ego. Psychologically, even if the spy acknowledges he is not working for a higher cause—and testimonies indicate that such is the case for a majority of them—ideology is a very useful moral cover and it helps spies justify their choices to their loved ones if they are ever exposed.

One double agent widely believed to have been motivated by ideology is Kim Philby, a member of the Cambridge Five: spies hailing from Trinity College at Cambridge University who betrayed their country and colleagues for the Soviet Union, fooling the UK and its intelligence services for decades. In his memoirs, Philby explains his choice, even if he suggests later on that his ideals were not as eagerly espoused by his masters: "I had already decided at nineteen, after a good look around me, that the rich had had it too damned good for too damned long and that the poor had had it too damned bad and it was time that it was all changed."

Not everyone believes that Philby's motivation was ideological. John Le Carré, the world-famous author of espionage novels and himself a spy who believed his cover was blown by Philby, said of the man: "Philby has no home, no woman, no faith. Behind the inbred upper-class arrogance, the taste for adventure, lies the self-hate of a vain misfit for whom nothing will ever be worthy of his loyalty. In the last instance, Philby is driven by the incurable drug of deceit itself."

Ana Montes, senior analyst at the US Defence Intelligence Agency (DIA), was also motivated by ideology to betray her country, spying for Cuba for more than sixteen years without any financial reward other than her regular salary paid by the US government.

Spy recruiters revere true ideologues because they are difficult to corrupt. The opposite is true, however, for counter-intelligence officers in search of foreign agents willing to betray their countries—ideologues in this case are reviled because it is hard to co-opt them. This somehow illustrates the perverse essence of espionage: 'anyone betraying my country is a traitor, unless he is betraying his own country in favour of my homeland, in which case he is a hero'.

Coercion, the 'C' in MICE, is often achieved through blackmail, and the number of potential recruits via this method is virtually limitless. This method is not only efficient; it is also the most widespread today. That's because it is unprecedentedly easy for a government, through surveillance and interception, to learn something the target may be embarrassed about, be it something as harmless as the category one chooses on a porn site, or a reckless comment about the attractive female friend of one's wife. Anyone who wants to keep a secret from even just one person, however small the peccadillo, can easily be blackmailed. Intelligence agencies have historically used many types of leverage to coerce people into spying, including knowledge about their sexual orientation, personal debt, or medical conditions. In certain areas of the Middle East, for example, where being gay can be deadly, homosexual spies are more likely to gather ammunition for blackmail, and are thus often posted to those regions. Female spies can be equally efficient when they seduce married politicians, policemen, and secret agents who would have their private lives destroyed by the disclosure of an extramarital affair.

Though often overlooked as potential motivations,

excitement and ego—the 'E' in MICE—are features appreciated by practically every spy. A secret agent who does not enjoy the thrill of his trade is like a surgeon who can't stand the sight of blood. For many agents, espionage is the culmination of their desire to live a life of crime while still being on the side of the law. In regard to ego, CIA psychiatrist Charney may surprise with the simplicity of his assessment: "I made a big discovery," he says. "I found the genetic marker for spies—the Y chromosome." Charney says that over ninety-five per cent of spies are men, and anyone with enough "male pride and ego" can fit the profile. It sounds peculiar, then, that the relationship between a spy and his handler often resembles that of a prostitute and a pimp.

Some of the most interesting and, by their nature, complicated relationships in a spy's life are those with his recruiters and handlers. In sourcing and motivating spies, recruiters and handlers establish a delicate balance of power. The essential techniques for creating bonds and boundaries are described by another illuminating acronym: RASCLS. It stands for Reciprocity, Authority, Scarcity, Commitment/Consistency and Liking. The concept of RASCLS was first developed by marketing expert Robert Cialdini in his book *Influence: Science and Practice*, a theory further validated in papers published by the CIA. Espionage and marketing, it turns out, have a core mandate in common: to persuade people to do something that may be against their best interest.

Recruiters, like in non-espionage fields, court their targets with:

Reciprocity. This involves making the recruit feel he is being taken care of, be it by issuing a visa for a family member, or giving them a box of their favourite chocolate. This will prompt the recruit to reciprocate. It is a type of social convention, a courtesy that becomes essential in the spy/handler relationship.

Authority works not only as a means of imposing respect, but creating a model to be admired and emulated by the recruited asset. The handler will also exert his authority by reinforcing his power to both improve, as well as destroy, the life of their operative.

Scarcity is about making a spy feel like they are being offered a gift, not a job, and that such an opportunity is fleeting and will not be offered again. For that, a recruiter should balance two ideas at the same time: that while the recruit is important, they are also replaceable.

Consistency. People do not like to be caught performing contradictory actions, which is where consistency and commitment come into play. This is particularly useful if the prospective spy has provided the handler with secret information: if they already did something, and considered it justified, they are more likely to keep doing it.

Liking, or a good rapport between handler and spy, is crucial for a long-term relationship. By the very nature of their work, spies are solitary people with few or no confidants, and a spy's connection with a handler may be the only long-term relationship they will have in a lifetime.

"The spy is the loneliest person in the world," says Charney. "When he crosses the line into spying, who can he talk to about that? Nobody except the handler." The handler, he says, exploits that situation, telling the recruit,

"You are gorgeous, you are lovely." It is, Charney explains, much like the relationship between a pimp and a prostitute. "Now and then, if they (spies and prostitutes) stray a little bit, the pimp is gonna put the fear of God into them. It's a mix of loving and control."

CHAPTER THREE

INTERVIEW PREPARATION: THE ELUSIVE ANSWER

"Describe your relationship with your mother." It sounds like a question posed by a therapist, or an awkward first date, but it's barely skimming the surface of the interrogation faced by would-be agents. In a rare glimpse of the recruiting process published on *FAS.org*, the website of the Federation of American Scientists, Ralph Perro (a pseudonym) reveals details of the interviews and security clearance he had to go through when he applied to work for the NSA, the US National Security Agency. As he says, the process was akin to "the most invasive medical procedure ending in '-oscopy'."

After completing an initial telephone interview, Perro was flown from San Francisco to Washington DC. In the atmosphere of secrecy established between him and his recruiter, he was urged not to mention the agency when booking his flight and hotel room—an unnecessary precaution, it turned out, when he saw the hotel sent him an email confirming his room-type as 'NSA'. According to Perro's description, "A few parts of the interview process were unintentionally more *Get Smart* than *Mission: Impossible*."

While waiting in the NSA lobby, Perro was made to answer a ten-page questionnaire in thirty minutes. He then was asked to take a computerized psychological exam with more than 500 True/False questions. He remembers some of them: "I would like the job of a forest ranger; I hear voices in my head; I read the crime reports in the newspaper; If someone has their possessions stolen from their unlocked car they had it coming." Other statements sounded more puzzling in their purpose, like: "I have a mortal fear of earthquakes; I have neck/hand pain; I like children." He was later interviewed by a psychologist and asked to describe his relationship with his parents, their own relationship between them, whether he had ever received psychological counselling, if he had attempted suicide, whether he abused any substances, how many drinks he had per week, when he first drank alcohol, and if he had ever stolen anything, among other questions. He was eventually handed a printout that declared him low to medium risk.

Throughout the process, Perro had no idea what the evaluation criteria were, or what were the correct answers for getting hired. Indeed, how can an intelligence agency assess one's loyalty when the job is essentially based on deceit? How can it gauge the potential trustworthiness of someone whom it expects to be eventually disloyal to acquaintances and friends, even family?

How can an intelligence agency assess one's loyalty when the job is essentially based on deceit? How can it gauge the potential trustworthiness of someone whom it expects to be eventually disloyal to acquaintances and friends, even family?

Perro passed enough stages to eventually take a polygraph, even though the test's credibility has been widely discredited. Aldrich Ames, for example, who spied for the Soviet Union for nine years from the top CIA position in Soviet counter-intelligence, was subjected to two lie detector examinations while he was actively betraying his country, and he passed both. Nonetheless, even though the polygraph does not indicate with any precision whether someone is lying or not, some believe the machine works in a roundabout way: people become so afraid of being caught telling a lie that they end up offering up information they otherwise wouldn't. Perro also went through a background investigation, and several of his neighbours and work colleagues were questioned about him. His application was eventually declined.

There is a pervading sentiment in the espionage business that no spy worth his mettle is actively recruited—the good ones have all been walk-ins, people who came to work for an agency on their own initiative and who may already possess secret information. The problem is that walk-ins are also more likely to be double agents. That's why the Force Research Unit branch of the British secret service decided to refuse any type of volunteer or walk-in. Britain's caution shouldn't be surprising, considering it hired and promoted Kim Philby to the top echelons of British intelligence. Philby, the most prolific traitor in the recent history of the United Kingdom, never hid his communist sympathies; quite the contrary—he boasted about them. "The ease of my entry surprised me," he wrote in his memoirs. It was so easy, in fact, that he and his befuddled Soviet contact thought he might have been accepted into the wrong organisation.

There is a pervading sentiment in the espionage business, that no spy worth his mettle is actively recruited—the good ones have all been walk-ins, people who came to work for an agency on their own initiative and who may already possess secret information. The problem is that walk-ins are also more likely to be double agents.

Amongst intelligence agencies, Mossad has a unique way of recruiting and forming its network, explained in detail by Ostrovsky and by Jacob Cohen, author of *Le Printemps des Sayanim*. It makes use of helpers all over the world, people often directly approached by them and unpaid for their services, who feel compelled to collaborate because of religious and ideological allegiances. Those helpers are recruited among Zionist Jews as sleeper agents: people who work at their regular jobs but who will be called for a mission as the need arises. When in 2004 Israeli spies Eli Cara and Uriel Kelman were sentenced in New Zealand for fraudulently obtaining a passport with the birth certificate of a man with cerebral palsy, it was revealed the plot was assisted by such local helpers, sayanim who owned businesses in the country and pretended those agents were their employees, providing them with local numbers and business cards. The three Mossad assassins sent to Damascus for the assassination of Hezbollah operative Imad Mughniyeh had covers provided by real people, sayanim who lent them their real background stories, professions, names, passports and even places of residence in France, Germany and Spain.

Ostrovsky was not a sayan, but a *katsa*, an agent intensively trained in real life situations before he is ready to be sent on a mission. In his gripping narrative, Ostrovsky recounts one of the tests he had to go through. His instructor takes him to a street in Tel Aviv and points at an apartment building, choosing a balcony at random: "I want you to first stand here for three minutes and think. Then I want you to go to that building and within six minutes, I want to see you standing out on the balcony with the owner or the tenant, holding a glass of water." Ostrovsky went to the apartment and told the 65-year-old woman who opened the door that he wanted to install a camera to monitor accidents at the intersection. On the balcony, he raised his glass of water to the man watching him from below.

Years later, that sort of quick thinking would come in handy. Ostrovsky had been assigned the task of going to a specific apartment and getting acquainted with one of the men inside. In the few minutes he had to complete the mission, Ostrovsky quickly bought two bottles of wine in a store nearby, ran to the building and rang a random buzzer to find out the name of a tenant who was absent in order to gain entry. He managed to get in and climbed the stairs, reaching the targeted apartment and smashing one of the bottles outside its door. He knocked, apologizing, and asked for something to clean up the mess. He then offered to share the other bottle, talking with his targets for two hours, soaking up their life stories and fully accomplishing his mission.

John Kiriakou, the CIA case officer who became a whistle-blower, describes in his book *The Reluctant Spy* that one of his training exercises involved having to catch, kill and skin a rabbit, and then eat it. He flunked it, letting the rabbit live. In *Deception*, Edward Lucas describes some of the exercises endured by trainees in Britain's Fort Monckton spy school: going to a pub and collecting personal information from people they never met; getting passport details; borrowing money from a stranger. "Some well brought-up trainees find this so demeaning that they quit," writes Lucas.

There in front of me was a man who could become my greatest interview yet, while he had in front of him possibly the only person he's ever met who sat with Hassan Nasrallah, arguably Israel's biggest enemy, someone Mossad had for decades tried to assassinate.

One prolific recruiter in US espionage was in fact a double agent recruiting other double agents for the USSR. John Anthony Walker, a US Navy chief warrant officer code-named 'Number 1' by the KGB, spied for the Russians for nearly two decades, selling them classified information and recruiting at least three other people into his spy ring: his brother, his son, and his best friend. He was arrested in 1985.

I may have myself been the target of one attempt at recruitment at the Counter-Terrorism conference in Herzliya in 2013, but I have no means of knowing if that was indeed the case. It was the third day of the terror masturbathon where one-trick ponies bent every possible theory, number, and logic into the need for more weapons. As someone with lofty concerns, I had gone to the organizers and complained that for the high price of admission they could have at least provided non-instant coffee to help the audience wash down that circus where every clown twisted his balloon into the same shape. On the third day, finally, the organisers listened. So, there I was, waiting in line for my turn at the espresso machine when a short, grey-haired man cuts the line right in front of me. I am often polite and considerate towards the elderly, but in that place my instinctive solicitude was nowhere to be found. As the man turned back to me smiling, cheeky, old-grandpa-style, I looked straight at him and said: "Normally I would send you to the back of the line, but in my country we have a dedicated queue for people your age." To my surprise, he replied in Lebanese-sounding Arabic. "Where did you learn it?" I asked. To my much bigger surprise, he said he had been Mossad's station chief in Lebanon and Iran.

I could hardly believe it: there in front of me was a man who could become my greatest interview yet, while he had in front of him possibly the only person he's ever met who sat with Hassan Nasrallah, arguably Israel's biggest enemy, someone Mossad had for decades tried to assassinate. That line-jumping couldn't have been a coincidence. Several thoughts rushed through my mind. I wondered whether I would ever be allowed back in Lebanon if I met this man privately. I speculated if my career—or life—would survive intact if an honest interview with him were to be published without his interference. I also thought of the several people who, while seeing me help feed beggars on Beirut's Bliss Street, warned me of the legendary Abu Rish: a homeless, malodorous man who would slowly walk up and down the street while locals helped him with food and clothing, only to one day watch Israeli tanks roll over Bliss and hand Abu Rish his real outfit, the uniform of the Israel Defence Forces.

My turn came for the coffee and the man was still there, beside me. At that moment, there were four simultaneous workshops taking place. I had chosen to attend Incitements to Terrorism, the one that featured the only Palestinian lecturer in the entire conference. I needed to see if anyone at that place would ever vent the crazy theory that perhaps the strongest motivation for terrorism is illegal occupation. As I walked to the room, Eliezer Tsafrir followed me, and I pondered over the odds of us choosing to attend the same conference. I sat down and he sat beside me while Itamar Marcus spoke about anti-Israeli indoctrination in Palestinian TV programs. Then he mis-translated 'crusaders' for 'Christians', and I impatiently interrupted to explain what should be obvious to any honest translator, that the word 'crusader' carries a connotation of territorial invasion absent in the word 'Christian'. Marcus dismissed that as an irrelevant nuance, and a man with a microphone announced that the Palestinian bit of the panel was cancelled, and the deceptively affable man beside me kept abu-rishingly begging for my attention and undue respect while I kept hearing the unbearable sound of lies and the clicking of metal made by the world's most stupidly-designed neck tags incessantly reverberating inside that little chamber of single-minded people, and I felt suffocated like I would among fanatics in a sect, and I headed to the door, leaving the conference long before the next coffee break.

Years later, I was contacted by a former colleague from Lebanon enquiring if I would consider working for a Hezbollah news outlet. I'd have some editorial freedom, he said. I was doubtful. *Al Akhbar*, frequently a Hezbollah mouthpiece, published an unflattering review of my book on Lebanese politics. They indeed didn't like my book, he explained, but they knew I was honest. "They don't have the means to know that," I said. "They know it," he insisted. "They know you've been approached, and that Mossad couldn't get you."

CHAPTER FOUR

TO CATCH A MOLE

The life of a double agent might seem rife with fear and paranoia, since they are surrounded by other spies, their own colleagues, the very people best trained to detect nefarious activities. Reality, however, shows that traitors have little to fear among the colleagues they betray, as most double agents are not caught by the people they deceive, but are instead eventually exposed by other double agents betraying the foreign intelligence with whom the former double agents collaborate. In other words, the people who know most about the intrigues going on in the dungeons of classified reality are two-timed by traitors in their midst, and they never find that out unless another traitor from an enemy agency gives, or sells, the incriminating information. It's spy versus spy versus spy going around an infinite wheel of betrayal. That is what happened with Robert Hanssen, named by the FBI as the most harmful double agent in the history of the Bureau.

Hanssen joined the FBI in 1976, and three years later got in touch with Soviet intelligence, offering the names of Russian officials he knew were secretly helping the US. That marked the beginning of a double agent career that would last for the next twenty-two years. During all that time, Hanssen never revealed his identity to the Russians, leaving garbage bags with classified documents and collecting his payment at 'dead drops': pre-arranged spots in public places where spies leave and pick up items without ever meeting in person.

Hanssen's father had been a Chicago policeman working in anti-communist intelligence. Hanssen himself was a member of Opus Dei, a very conservative right-wing branch of the Catholic Church. He is said to have become more religiously fervent as his betrayal continued on, and he confessed his treason to his priest several times. While his main motivation is hard to determine, the estimated $600,000 he received from Russia must have played a part. According to *Time* magazine, when Hanssen started selling information to the Russians, the average salary of an FBI agent in New York was so low that some of them needed food stamps. Regardless of the money, the pull of excitement and ego must have been very significant. The risk of being caught was particularly high, considering that for many years the Bureau was headed by Louis Freeh, who not only attended the same church as Hanssen, but also had his children in the same school. In two decades of betrayal, Freeh never suspected a thing.

In 1990, Hanssen's brother-in-law, also an FBI agent, reported him when he noticed Hanssen's wealth could not be explained by his salary. The warning, despite coming from someone so close, was ignored. Hanssen was also caught twice flunking security rules. One time, caught red-handed trying to hack into a colleague's computer, Hanssen managed to get away by saying that he was trying to prove the system was vulnerable. While he kept passing American secrets to Russia, the FBI suspected there was a leak but suspected the wrong agent, an innocent man who ended up being investigated for two years. Meanwhile, Hanssen's treason was causing serious damage, and at least two Russian moles collaborating with the United States were executed because of his disclosures. He also revealed something still today unknown to many of Washington's inhabitants: a 600-foot-long illegal spy tunnel built by the US government under the Soviet embassy.

Frustrated with the lack of leads, the FBI allegedly offered one of its Russian assets $7 million for information. The informant couldn't find out Hanssen's name, but he eventually provided the FBI with a recording of the traitor talking to his Russian handler, along with some of the bags used in the dead drops still carrying Hanssen's fingerprints. The FBI put Hanssen under surveillance and eventually caught him making a dead drop in a park in 2001. As he was being handcuffed, Hanssen turned to the FBI agents and asked: "What took you so long?"

Aldrich Ames, the US turncoat whose damage is second only to that inflicted by Hanssen, also worked in Soviet counter-intelligence, this time for the CIA. In that position, he was naturally in contact with Russian officials betraying the KGB. In early 1985, while the Cold War was raging, Ames sold to the Russians a list of their traitors assisting the United States. For the next nine years, Ames amassed more than $4 million as payment for classified information, while CIA officials watched with dismay as their assets in Russia started to disappear, get arrested, or be executed.

At that time, CIA's espionage in Russia was so pervasive that officers joked that the Agency had not just one station at the US embassy in Moscow but two more: one at the KGB headquarters and another at the offices of GRU, the military intelligence. But then, CIA assets started to get caught. In August 1985, a counter-intelligence Russian agent stationed in Nigeria who had been collaborating with the CIA for more than ten years was arrested in Moscow. A few months later, another Russian agent helping the CIA in Lisbon was arrested. One by one, double agents started falling. In July 1986, retired general Dmitri Polyakov was arrested. He was known as the 'crown jewel' of collaborators and had been spying for the CIA for over twenty years. Hanssen had already warned the Russians about Polyakov, but the warning was ignored. With Ames's confirmation, the man was finally executed.

Two CIA officials, Sandra Grimes and Jeanne Vertefeuille, are widely credited with identifying Ames. In their book *Circle of Treason*, they explain they caught Ames through a very unorthodox, unscientific method they devised: they asked some colleagues to make a list of people they suspected of being the mole. They then ascribed a numerical value to each name according to their position in the lists, from most to least suspected. Even though Ames was on top of only one of the lists, he was present in most of them, and his 'suspicion score' was the highest. Grimes and Vertefeuille communicated the findings to their superiors, but the CIA didn't immediately take action, and like the FBI had done with Hanssen, it missed many clues and opportunities to arrest the right culprit.

Other cases were easier to crack, and mostly not due to great tradecraft on one side, but to lack of it on the other. In 2010, 28-year-old Anna Chapman, a woman spying for Russia, was caught in Manhattan after an undercover FBI agent offered her a forged passport, which she allegedly accepted. In a form she had filled in for a temporary telephone number, Chapman stated her address as 99 Fake Street. Because she had no official cover, in other words she was not a Russian diplomat, Chapman had no legal immunity and was therefore arrested and tried. She was eventually deported to Russia in a prisoner exchange. In 2013, it was the turn of an American spy to play Agent 86 in Russia. Ryan Christopher Fogle, who *did* have diplomatic cover, was tackled by the Russian police in Moscow and handcuffed after trying to co-opt an agent from the FSB (a spin-off of the KGB) with $100,000 in cash. Fogle was wearing an unconvincing blond wig while carrying a compass, a Swiss army knife and a letter addressing the prospective double agent. The letter started with "This is a down payment from someone who is very impressed with your professionalism, and who would greatly appreciate your collaboration in the future." The written document went on to promise payments of up to $1 million per year for information. That in itself reveals quite bluntly the spirit of espionage: if the average income of a CIA agent is about $90,000 per year, and treason is rewarded with $1 million, it is rendered numerically clear that the US government values a traitor more than it does an honest worker.

CHAPTER FIVE

A VERY BRIEF HISTORY OF ESPIONAGE

If popular legend has it that prostitution is the oldest profession, espionage may well be the second oldest. In fact, one of the most ancient narratives in the world relates a story featuring both occupations. The Book of Joshua tells of Rahab, a harlot from Jericho who managed an inn. The Israelites, encamped at Shittim, sent two spies to assess Jericho's defences before their attack. The king attempted to capture the spies, but Rahab hid them under piles of flax put out to dry on the roof of her inn. For her collaboration, Rahab and her family had their lives spared when the Israelites invaded the town and "utterly destroyed all that was in the city, both man and woman, both young and old, and ox, and sheep, and ass, with the edge of the sword." In one of the greatest honours in Jewish culture, Rahab is enshrined in Hebrews 11, known as the biblical Hall of Faith, and is the only other woman mentioned in that chapter except Abraham's wife, Sarah.

In the fifth century BC, Chinese philosopher, general, and military strategist Sun Tzu described five types of spies in *The Art of War*, all of them still widely used in modern espionage. A 'local' spy is one hired from amongst the people that will be spied upon. An 'inside' spy is someone well placed within enemy ranks, preferably an official—now commonly known as a 'mole'. A 'reverse' spy is a double agent, an enemy spy that switches sides and reports on his former employers. A 'dead' spy is someone sent with false information to deceive the enemy, a ruse that when discovered will probably result in the spy's death. Finally, a 'living' spy is one who manipulates others but is never manipulated, fooled or seduced into betrayal, successfully coming back to his territory with intelligence. For Sun Tzu, the use of espionage was morally justified because good intelligence could prevent wars and save lives. Throughout history, however, espionage has been used to promote and prolong wars.

Alexander the Great's spy networks counted enemy troops at night as part of battle preparations. Generals in the Roman Empire employed surveillance, eavesdropping, disguises, and *agent provocateurs* to incite rebellions. Centuries later, the Aztecs made use of the *pochteca*, a class of merchants who travelled long distances under diplomatic cover for economic espionage.

In sixteenth century Elizabethan England, Secretary of State Francis Walsingham helped pioneer decryption techniques and a method of breaking and restoring wax seals. He is credited with foiling a conspiracy to assassinate Queen Elizabeth, a Protestant, by her cousin, Mary, Queen of Scots, a Catholic. Mary was living in a sort of house arrest imposed by Elizabeth, and was forbidden from sending or receiving letters. Walsingham led Mary to believe her communications with co-conspirators were safely secreted away in beer kegs. Instead, they were intercepted, decoded, and resealed by Walsingham, who gathered enough evidence to send Mary to the gallows.

It wasn't until complex state bureaucracies combined with the imperialist ambitions of the modern age that espionage evolved from a tool of government into a quasi-government of its own. That reality became most pronounced during The Great Game, the protracted struggle between the Russian and British empires initiated in the turn of the nineteenth century for the domination of Central Asia. For more than a hundred years, the two empires sought to control and exploit Afghanistan, India, Iran, and other countries rich in natural resources and of strategic geopolitical importance. The complexity of having to build alliances, wage proxy wars, and plan subterfuges from thousands of miles away required a more professional intelligence infrastructure than either country possessed. It was during this period that espionage was assigned a permanent role.

The Austrian Empire was the first to establish a military intelligence service, the Evidenzbureau, in 1850. In Britain, military espionage began to be conducted by the government department responsible for topographic measurement and statistics during the Crimean War (1853–1856). France's Ministry of War created the Deuxième Bureau in 1871, and Germany, Italy, and Russia followed suit with their own versions. With the creation of dedicated intelligence agencies, spying ceased to be a concealed weapon and

With the creation of dedicated intelligence agencies, spying ceased to be a concealed weapon and became an acceptable political instrument, and the machinations done in the shadows were now part of everyday governance.

became an acceptable political instrument, and the machinations done in the shadows were now part of everyday governance. No longer under the authority and restraint of military and naval offices, espionage grew its own civilian branches in the most powerful European countries. The MI6 and MI5, for example, respectively the foreign and domestic espionage agencies in the United Kingdom, were originally two branches of military intelligence. By the beginning of the twentieth century, intelligence agencies had firmly entrenched themselves as part of the existing political bureaucracy.

As the use of espionage expanded, new agencies were created to counter the work of foreign spies, a solution creating more problems for it to solve, a self-regurgitating ouroboros. It was within this new amalgam of politics, deception, mistrust, and betrayal that a French housekeeper at the German embassy in Paris found a handwritten message torn into pieces in 1894 and decided to give it to French counter-intelligence, triggering the Dreyfus Affair, an event that split public opinion in France, and one of the biggest espionage mishaps in history. Alfred Dreyfus, a Jewish officer in the French army, was falsely accused of passing information to the Germans. The evidence was scant, however, and the trial shoddy. Subsequent investigations identified Major Walsin Esterhazy as the mole, but it took ten whole years for Dreyfus's name to be cleared.

Throughout the nineteenth and twentieth centuries, international and domestic political allegiances grew more complex, and intelligence bureaucracies trained their sights on internal targets as a matter of course rather than exception. The Russian Okhrana, for example, persecuted

Established in 1947, the CIA marked the inception of the deep state, an unelected group of officials that have ruled virtually without oversight and sometimes without government approval, a permanent underground bureaucracy that remains in power regardless of election results.

domestic dissent through sabotage, false-flag operations and widespread surveillance of the Bolsheviks.

The First and Second World Wars became a major testing ground for espionage techniques. One of the simplest, and yet most efficient stratagems was the monitoring of railways, allowing the military to learn about the transportation of supplies, weapons, and the movement of troops. Intelligence may also have prompted the United States to declare war on Germany in World War I, after British agents intercepted an internal communication between German Foreign Secretary Arthur Zimmermann to the German ambassador in Mexico. In the coded telegram, Zimmermann was offering to help Mexico regain its territories of Texas, Arizona, and New Mexico from the United States.

The Cold War between the US and the Soviet Union was fertile ground for espionage, as conventional battles were largely replaced by intrigue, sabotage, and proxy conflicts in countries aligned with either the USSR or the US. By then, the Central Intelligence Agency had already been created, replacing the old Office of Strategic Services (OSS). Established in 1947, the CIA didn't simply represent a change in acronym—it marked the inception of the deep state, an unelected group of officials that have ruled virtually without oversight and sometimes without government approval, a permanent underground bureaucracy that remains in power regardless of election results. More than ever before, there began an irrefutable rupture between public government and secret governance, between appearance and reality.

A conspiracy theory, it is said, is a truth that hasn't yet been proven—not least because the truth is often protected by law. The US government has the legal right to hide information from the public for decades, a practice common in several other countries. With the outsourcing of war and intelligence to private companies, it has become even easier for the government to cover up and manipulate reality, among other reasons because contractors facilitate what in legal defence is known as 'plausible deniability': the ability of public officials to deny knowledge or responsibility for a misdeed and, by virtue of that, evade the chain of command. Several examples of the latter occurred in Iraq, when mercenaries of Black Water committed war crimes, but could not be tried by a military court because they were civilians. And, because they were civilians, the military officers above them could not be considered responsible for their violations. The outsourcing to private companies of government intelligence promotes conspiracy theories in a myriad of other ways. The argument that it is harder to keep a criminal conspiracy from the public when private companies are involved does not stand up to scrutiny.

One remarkable case, still surprisingly unknown to the public at large, is the story of Nayirah. On 10 October 1990, a 15-year-old Kuwaiti girl, known simply as Nayirah, gave her testimony to a human rights caucus at the US Congress about how she witnessed the Iraqi army invade a maternity ward in Kuwait and throw the babies out of their incubators, leaving them for dead. That perfectly graphic event became the ideal impetus for a war against Iraq. George Bush Sr mentioned it twice before he declared war on the country. Amnesty International condemned the crime, and the terrifying story was replicated in news bulletins throughout the world. Two years later, it was revealed that Nayirah was actually a member of the Kuwaiti royal family, and had told a story fully fabricated by the PR company Hill & Knowlton.

More recently, the 2011 capture of Osama Bin Laden may not have been a capture at all. Lauded in the news and in the movie theatres as 'history's greatest manhunt for the world's most dangerous man', according to the official version, the operation was a remarkable effort of espionage that revealed Bin Laden's hideout and culminated in the Operation Neptune Spear: a raid on his lair in Abbottabad by a team of Navy SEALS, who killed him and disposed of his body in the sea. But the well-respected journalist Seymour Hersh says reality was very different and much less cinematographic. According to his investigation, the Pakistani Secret Service had been keeping Osama Bin Laden under house arrest since 2006, if not longer. And the US government did not discover this through a long and formidable espionage mission either but, again, through that most unsophisticated of manners: it learned of Bin Laden's whereabouts via the betrayal of an agent of another espionage outfit, who offered to exchange the information for money.

CHAPTER SIX

TANGLED WEBS

In 1997, the US government declassified documents related to Operation Northwoods, a 1962 plot devised by the Department of Defence and the Joint Chiefs of Staff to carry out a series of terrorist attacks on American soil to kill innocent civilians, hijack planes, blow up ships, and sink boats carrying Cuban refugees—all to be blamed on Fidel Castro. The attacks were meant to justify a war with Cuba, but President John F. Kennedy vetoed the plan. He did, however, authorize Operation Mongoose, a set of thirty-three black ops in Cuba that included economic sabotage, destruction of crops, anti-Castro propaganda, and the bombing of harbours. The operation went as far as envisioning a way to make Castro's beard fall out, and contaminating a TV studio with hallucinogens just before the Cuban leader recorded a televised speech, in order to interfere with his performance. Despite being fully

Britain's main goal was to prevent the migration of Jewish people to Palestine, then under British control, by fitting refugee boats with explosives and thus discourage it. As an official document stated, the plan of intimidation "is only likely to be effective if some members of the group of people to be intimidated actually suffer unpleasant consequences."

documented, those plots are still widely ignored by the very people on whose names they were planned.

In 2010, historian Keith Jeffery was allowed to examine the historical archives of Britain's foreign espionage service, research which resulted in an astoundingly revealing book. In *The Secret History of MI6: 1909-1949*, Jeffery notes a conspicuous absence of documents relating to the Holocaust, an unlikely coincidence that indicates they may have long since been destroyed by the MI6. But among the later records that were not destroyed, Jeffery found evidence of a plan whose atrocity defies belief.

The aptly named Operation Embarrass was a model of astounding perfidy, but also a masterpiece among false-flag operations, as it managed to hit several targets in one single strike. Britain's main goal was to prevent the migration of Jewish people to Palestine, then under British control, by fitting refugee boats with explosives and thus discourage it. As an official document stated, the plan of intimidation "is only likely to be effective if some members of the group of people to be intimidated actually suffer unpleasant consequences." Jeffery takes pains to stress that the government wanted to avoid casualties, and if the book is any indication, there were no deaths but several boats were sunk or rendered unseaworthy. The operation also took care to cause damage to other countries in its crosshairs by using their harbours, or explosives ostensibly manufactured by their national industry.

Britain decided that the attacks would be blamed on Palestinians, and created a fake group to claim authorship, the Defenders of Arab Palestine. Letters sent to high government officials and newspapers from the fake

Palestinian group were typed on typewriters of 'appropriate nationality' and posted in Paris. Britain also used this opportunity to incriminate the Soviets by stating in the letters that Russia was trying to force the establishment of a communist Jewish state. To further prod the Soviets to act against Jewish migration, Britain left in a Vienna nightclub frequented by Russian agents forged UK documents stating that, "Jewish migrants from behind the iron-curtain were a valuable source of information on Russian activities in that area." The boats to be sabotaged were to sail from France and Italy, harming those two countries in the process (eventually only boats sailing from Italian ports were used). When the boat famously known as *Exodus 1947* was seized by Britain in Palestine and its 4,500 refugees were sent back, an MI6 officer lamented over how much that was bad PR for Britain and great publicity for the Zionists: "[That] could have been spared if the Foreign Office had permitted the SIS [MI6] to take the appropriate action against the [ship] when they suggested doing so."

The invasion of Finland by the Soviets was based on a false-flag event. On 26 November 1939, a Soviet guard post on the border with Finland near the town of Mainila was shelled and four Russian guards were killed. It was later found out that the Soviet Union killed its own men in order to justify an invasion of Finland.

The perfect false-flag mission will fulfil several goals at once, and get rid of Enemy A while blaming Enemy B for the crime. But false flags have another pernicious, widespread effect that has been sadly left unexamined: they help muddle reliable political analysis by falsely designating victims as culprits, and vice-versa, fudging political scenarios, distorting reality, and creating an insidious and stubborn sense that truth is unattainable.

The purview of espionage includes more than picturesque dead drops, wiretapping, and phone shoes. It also entails black ops, covert action, sabotage, disruption of financial markets, psychological operations, propaganda, and assassinations. Most of those types of action are assigned their respective departments in the main secret agencies around the world. Espionage also involves manoeuvres that are less violent but still harmful, like CIA's Operation Mockingbird, a secret 1950s plot to sway the public in favour of the CIA and its political leanings. The agency achieved its goal by bribing journalists and having its own reports published as if they were the work of genuine newspaper reporters. Operation Mockingbird also included the funding of magazines and the creation of student and cultural associations.

Intelligence agencies, largely impervious to oversight, can commit appalling crimes without legal consequences. Secrecy is often protected by law, and occasional liability is rendered null by keeping the chain of command of an operation purposely blurred.

The protective cloak of plausible deniability can extend as high as the US President, who may be kept deliberately ignorant of a CIA plot so as to keep them immune from guilt if the operation is perchance exposed. Other times, he may do just like Ronald Reagan, and allege (as Steve Coll in the book *Ghost Wars* claims) that he could not understand the briefings of CIA Director William Casey.

"My problem with Bill was that I didn't understand him at meetings. [...] So I'd just nod my head, but I didn't know what he was actually saying." US Defence Secretary Robert McNamara also said that while he negotiated the Cuban missile crisis with the Soviet Nikita Khrushchev he didn't know that the CIA had tried to assassinate Fidel Castro.

Sometimes the agency will act on its own, or it will wait for the right moment. In the case of Operation Ajax, the CIA presented the plan to President Harry Truman but he opposed it. The CIA then just waited for Dwight Eisenhower to take over, and carried out Ajax under his administration. The secret plot, devised in tandem with British intelligence, aimed at overthrowing Mohammad Mosaddegh, the popular Iranian Prime Minister who had been elected on an unprecedented platform of secularism, social justice and equality, vowing to fight both the corruption of the secular rule of Reza Pahlavi, as well as the undemocratic and retrograde power of the clergy. More importantly, Mosaddegh promised to nationalize the Iranian oil industry, for decades controlled by Britain.

The weight of the British yoke was heavy and inhumane. The refinery town of Abadan, where Iranian workers lived, was a squalid shanty town with no electricity or running water. They often got sick, but they had no paid leave. Working for one of the most profitable oil companies in the world, on their own soil, Iranians were refused access to buses reserved for the British, who frequented clubs that bore signs that read "Dogs and Iranians are not allowed."

According to the gripping non-fiction account *All the Shah's Men* by Stephen Kinzer, in order to persuade the Shah to join the coup, the CIA operative Kermit

Roosevelt Jr. had to convince Pahlavi that its MI6 British counterpart was in on it. To that end, Roosevelt told the Shah there would be a discreet but identifying sign from Britain to demonstrate its participation in the overthrow of Mosaddegh: a simple change in the way the BBC signed off the day's broadcast, requested by Winston Churchill himself. Indeed, on the assigned night, instead of "It is now midnight" the BBC Radio ended its program with "It is now *exactly* midnight." The CIA also bribed Pahlavi's sister with mink coats and money to convince her brother to participate. It organised marches and demonstrations against Mosaddegh, distributing pamphlets and provoking riots. The press was bought or simply coerced into writing against the Prime Minister, calling him a communist and accusing him of secretly being a Jew. Some articles were signed by local journalists, but written in Washington. According to Richard Cottam, a Harvard PhD who worked for the State Department in the Middle East, at the height of the coup, four out of five Iranian newspapers were under the control of the CIA. With all that concerted effort, Operation Ajax succeeded, extinguishing any hopes of democratic change with the toppling of Mosaddegh, the return of the Shah, and the eventual victory of the religious elite with the installation of Ayatollah Khomeini.

The CIA has a dedicated department for covert operations, the Special Activities Division, under which it conducts paramilitary operations and clandestine political action, or 'black ops'. Paramilitary members of this force don't wear a uniform, so the government can deny knowledge of their existence if they are captured or compromised. Through clandestine operations, the CIA has helped or directly caused the enthroning of some of the world's worst tyrants. It has also helped destroy the hopes of some of the most promising democratic leaders. According to the thorough research of many a serious author, the CIA may not only have been aware that John F. Kennedy was going to be assassinated, but indeed taken part in it. The plot would have been engendered by Allen Dulles, who had been the longest-serving CIA Director and a key member from its inception until the unthinkable happened: he was fired by Kennedy. Hated by Kennedy and hating him in return, Dulles was nonetheless the man appointed to head the investigation of JFK's assassination.

The NSA, the most powerful of the seventeen agencies in the US intelligence community, also conducts covert activities. The fact that so many agencies perform similar and overlapping work is yet another way of smudging liability, and keeping the structure so bloated and blurred it starts to function as a government of its own.

Despite all the power and funds dedicated to intelligence agencies, their failures are innumerable, and those failures can mean the death of innocent people. In 2016 alone, the intelligence budget of the US was a staggering 70.7 billion dollars, but even with all that tax money spent year after year on espionage, the US never anticipated the fall of the Berlin Wall, the Arab Spring, or the succession of North Korea's Kim Jong-il. The CIA, dubbed by some the Central Lack of Intelligence Agency, was well established in Iran, and yet it allegedly failed to anticipate the Iranian

Through clandestine operations, the CIA has helped or directly caused the enthroning of some of the world's worst tyrants. It has also helped destroy the hopes of some of the most promising democratic leaders.

Revolution, one of the biggest political events of the twentieth century. In fact, the CIA famously announced, only six months before, that "Iran is not in a revolutionary or even a pre-revolutionary situation." US intelligence didn't prevent Pearl Harbour either, or the 9/11 attacks, the Boston Marathon bombing, nor the massacre of thirteen people inside the military post of Fort Hood—even though the shooter had been exchanging emails with a radical Yemeni cleric who was being monitored by US intelligence. The Soviet invasion of Afghanistan in 1979 also took the US by surprise. The 2003 US invasion of Iraq, justified on faulty intelligence, cost the US tax payer an estimated $2 trillion and hundreds of thousands of civilian and military lives, all wasted in an effort to destroy an arsenal that never really existed.

The London Underground and bus bombings of July 2005 were another testament to intelligence failure—or so at least it appears. Conclusions to who-knew-what got very muddled a few hours after the attack, known as 7/7, when Peter Power, a crisis management specialist who owned Visor Consultants, gave an interview to Peter Allen of BBC Radio 5. Sounding agitated and in disbelief, Power told the BBC that his firm was simulating attacks at the very same Underground stations where the bombings took place, at the very same time. "We were actually running an exercise for a company of over a thousand people in London based on simultaneous bombs going off precisely at the railway stations where it happened this morning. I still have the hairs on the back of my neck standing upright," he told Allen, explaining that "for obvious reasons" he could not reveal the name of the company that hired his firm, "but they are listening and they will know it." It is well accepted in the espionage industry that security drills make for the most efficient covers in case an operation is bungled, because they explain away the otherwise unexplainable: the equipment, the explosives, the personnel in place.

Ironically—or so one hopes—the terrorist attacks in London took place right under the nose of a CIA veteran. Bob Kiley had made headlines in 2001, when he became the first American to ever be appointed for the highly prestigious position of London Commissioner for Transport. The fact that an American would head London Transport was so unlikely the BBC called it a "sea-change in British culture." It reported that Kiley had not only been a public transit expert with experience in Boston and New York, but also a CIA agent for years, having "travelled the world in the 1960s fighting communism and spying on radical students before settling down as the executive assistant to that most frigid of all Cold War warriors, the director of central intelligence, Richard Helms."

Kiley left the job not long after the London attacks, before his term was over, but still kept his salary and the $2.6 million mansion Transport for London got him. With virtually no work other than nominal consultancy, drinking heavily and complaining of idleness, Kiley was however receiving what is believed to have been at the time the highest pay for a public servant in the UK.

Although the CIA is a favourite inspiration for spy movies and novels, the most powerful espionage outfit in the US is the National Security Agency, the NSA. Formally founded in 1952, its creation was classified, and members of the intelligence community used to expand the acronym as *No Such Agency*. Its mission, as officially stated, is to "collect (including through clandestine means), process, analyse, produce, and disseminate signals, intelligence information, and data." In less abstract terms, the NSA hacks computers, bugs equipment, intercepts phone calls, rigs underwater fibre optic cables, and stores data about almost everyone, almost everywhere in the world. Its employees were caught physically intercepting routers, servers, and other computer hardware in equipment as widely sold as Cisco, inserting NSA Trojan horses before the devices were shipped to customers.

After the document trove leaked by Edward Snowden, an NSA contractor working at Booz Allen, the world finally confirmed the suspicion that the NSA illegally engages in economic espionage in spite of the US Economic Espionage Act of 1996. In France, for example, the NSA intercepted communications of the Finance Minister and every company negotiating contracts worth more than $200 million. The NSA also tapped the personal phones of several world leaders from allied countries, like the President of Brazil and the German Chancellor, and it spied on companies like Brazilian oil giant Petrobras.

Such unbridled surveillance may help catch terrorists, but it can also make terrorists of its own by providing individuals within NSA and its outsourced firms the power to subject anyone to blackmail. Intelligence agencies and less intelligent people like to say that if you haven't committed a crime, you have nothing to fear. But that is preposterous. Anyone can be blackmailed as long as a secret needs to be kept from a specific person: a visit to a porn site, a lewd comment about a sister-in-law, the existence of a mistress, a homosexual inclination, etc. The truth of that statement has been established at least since 2003 by no less than the NSA and GCHQ, its counterpart agency in the UK, when it was revealed that they attempted to eavesdrop on members of the UN Security Council to blackmail the diplomats into voting for the invasion of Iraq. Endorsed by George Bush and Tony Blair, the incredibly contemptible ploy only came to light thanks to the courage of whistle-blower Katharine Gun, a linguist working for GCHQ.

The NSA and GCHQ are part of the Five Eyes, a consortium of collaborating agencies from the US, UK, Canada, Australia and New Zealand that share intelligence with each other. There is, however, one catch to that misleadingly gracious communion among those independent nations: foreign intelligence agencies are legally prevented from spying on their own citizens, but with the Five Eyes, they each spy on each other's nationals and share the goods, effectively breaking the law without technically doing so.

But there's another dark aspect to the work of the NSA that is hardly ever discussed. While it probes inside private lives, acquiring the means to destroy them, the NSA can also protect the public work of civil servants and elected officials by reserving the right to classify anything about them, from evidence of corruption to official documents and daily bureaucratic procedures. It's an almost unbelievable scenario, unimaginable in a true democracy: private lives become fair game, while the public work of representatives of the people can be concealed from the very people they represent.

CHAPTER SEVEN

AGENTS OF DUPLICITY

Espionage and counter-espionage are traditionally carried out by separate agencies. In the US, espionage is conducted by the CIA, which sends its spies abroad, while counter-espionage is a job for the FBI, which protects the homeland from being a target of precisely the same thing the CIA sets out to do in other countries. But in the derailed gravy train of US espionage, while foreign intelligence trespasses its mandate engaging in domestic spying, the FBI goes way beyond its borders to incite cyber crimes against foreign countries.

According to documents revealed by journalist Dell Cameron of *The Daily Dot*, the high-profile hacking of the Texas-based intelligence firm Stratfor, which resulted in the theft of credit card numbers and associated data of 60,000 clients and millions of their emails was, in fact, monitored, allowed, and possibly instigated by the FBI, with the help of its informant, Hector Xavier Monsegur. Sabu, as the informer is known among hackers, also attacked the sites of companies and government departments in Turkey, Nigeria, Pakistan, Syria, Iran, and Brazil, all while working for the Bureau.

Questioned about its participation in Sabu's crimes, an FBI spokesperson released a statement to *Motherboard* saying among other things, "We've been involved in cyber crimes for a while now so we've been in the forefront of that, so I think the FBI is well positioned to conduct cyber ." The security company Symantec says there's been a rapid increase in bank heists through electronic means. In 2016, $80 million were stolen from Bangladesh's central bank with the use of computers alone. Other electronic crimes are also on the rise. Ransomware, a type of cyber attack that extorts money from victims under threat of having their personal information revealed, increased by 266%, and affected about 463,000 people in 2016. While some believe the FBI is "well positioned to conduct cyber investigations," others find the words "we've been involved in cyber crimes for a while now" a bit more compelling. In other cases, some of them quite sinister, there is less doubt about the FBI's role in instigating crime, rather than investigating it.

Beyond counter-espionage, the FBI is also tasked with counterterrorism, an activity given unprecedented importance after the 9/11 attacks. It may surprise many people, therefore, to learn that the FBI is also responsible for "hatching and financing more terrorist plots in the United States than any other group." That is the conclusion of an investigation conducted by the journalist Trevor

Aaronson, author of *The Terror Factory: Inside the FBI's Manufactured War on Terrorism*.

Since 9/11, the FBI has investigated hundreds of cases related to terrorism, parading suspects in front of cameras and showing the world how the Bureau is keeping America safe. In the first ten years after 9/11, more than 508 people were prosecuted in federal terrorism-related cases. What many Americans don't know is that a large part of those cases were actually created by the FBI through sting operations. Sting operations are deceptive undertakings aimed at catching criminals by first instigating them to commit a crime. Those procedures are so morally questionable that they are illegal in most developed nations.

Based on official FBI data, Aaronson found that of the 508 cases of so-called terrorism, about 250 of them involved people who were charged with simply lying to the FBI or violating immigration rules, and who were not related to anyone involved in any type of terrorism plot. Another 150 defendants were caught in sting operations that Aaronson says, "were solely the creation of the FBI." Those plots were either led by an FBI informant or an undercover agent who found potential targets—mostly men without any criminal record who were often mentally ill or in desperate economic situation—and provided them with everything necessary to commit the crime: the partners, the financial reward, the equipment, sometimes even the idea. Indeed, only six of the 508 people prosecuted had connections to terrorism and possessed weapons that were acquired without the help of the FBI. Most damningly, none of the six were caught by the FBI before they attempted the attack.

An agency that benefits so much from terror must make sure taxpayers perceive terror as a widespread threat, even though the most tangible consequence of terrorism is the terror spread by the fear of it.

Money seems to be at the root of the FBI's crime-fighting-gone-wild. Its annual budget for counterterrorism alone is around $3.3 billion, yet it gets only $2.6 billion to investigate all other crimes combined, including financial fraud, government corruption, and organised crime. An agency that benefits so much from terror must make sure taxpayers perceive terror as a widespread threat, even though the most tangible consequence of terrorism is the terror spread by the fear of it. According to FBI's own official data, an American is more likely to be killed by lightning than in a terrorist attack.

While demonstrably incompetent at catching criminals, the FBI is extremely good at hiring them. In California it employed an informant named Craig Monteilh, a felon convicted on drug charges. Under the fake Arab name of Farouk al-Aziz, he would search mosques in pursuit of radical Muslims while pretending to be one himself. He never came up with anything, but he harassed so many Muslims with his alleged sympathy for terrorists that his targeted recruits got a restraining order against him.

Most FBI informants are criminals or conmen hoping to get a reduction on their sentence, and many of them are paid real money for their collaboration. The life of an informant can be very lucrative, and some payments are known to have reached $400,000. The FBI has currently about 15,000 registered informants. In 2002, informant Robert Childs helped the FBI catch Abu Khalid, Abdul-Latif and Walli Mujahidh, accused of plotting an attack on a Seattle military recruiting centre. But Aaronson questions their conviction, because the weapons used in

The rampant pursuit of potential criminals, terrorists, and traitors has many watchdogs asking how many of those people would have ever turned terrorists were it not for the prodding of FBI covert agents.

the plot were provided by the FBI, and both men had been diagnosed with mental illness. In a secret conversation between agents, recorded by mistake and leaked to the press, one agent commenting on the operation is heard doubting the efficacy of their scheme: "I'm trying to think, if I'm a retarded fool who is hard-up for money and I don't have a pot to piss in, another five hundred dollars looks pretty good."

It's impossible to know with certainty if these men would have attempted even a misdemeanour without the FBI's prodding, but the crimes of the paid informant are not in doubt—Robert Childs is a sex offender convicted of child molestation and two counts of rape. And yet, for helping the FBI arrest two men who may otherwise have never thought of committing a crime, the rapist was paid $90,000.

Sometimes, instead of using tax payers' money as a recruitment tool, the FBI uses blackmail. The FBI often coerces immigrants seeking visas or trying to get family members to America, pressuring them into collaborating with the Bureau. Many of those recruits are Muslim, targeted because they can easily be threatened with deportation or arbitrary arrest. The Associated Press revealed that the NYPD asked the New York taxi commission to report "on all the city's Pakistani cab drivers, looking for those who got licenses fraudulently and might be susceptible to pressure to cooperate."

The rampant pursuit of potential criminals, terrorists, and traitors has many watchdogs asking how many of those people would have ever turned terrorists were it not for the prodding of FBI covert agents. "I've come to the conclusion," Aaronson says, "that the FBI is much better at creating terrorists than it is at catching them." In the case known as Newburgh Four—involving four men entrapped by the FBI in a poor neighbourhood rife with crime—the informant promised one of the defendants $250,000, a new BMW, a barber shop, and a holiday in Puerto Rico—a windfall that most successful crimes in real life could not match. The FBI also offered thousands of dollars to the other men, one of whom had such serious mental issues that he kept bottles of his own urine at home.

Meanwhile, the FBI failed to anticipate the Boston Marathon attacks, even though it had Tamerlan Tsarnaev on file. It also didn't catch Faisal Shahzad, whose plot to detonate a car bomb in New York's Times Square was foiled when two street vendors reported seeing smoke coming out of the vehicle. According to former FBI special-agent-turned-whistle-blower Coleen Rowley, the FBI could have prevented the attacks on 9/11 altogether, had it heeded a very solid tip on Zacarias Moussaoui, a man widely believed to have worked in cahoots with the hijackers. The tip had come from the Minneapolis police investigation, and identified Moussaoui as a terrorist learning to fly planes. Rowley's allegations against a possible cover-up became public through a letter she addressed to the then FBI Director Robert Mueller, called by a *Time* magazine cover story "the bombshell memo".

The use of informants in the professed fight against domestic terrorism is also growing in Britain, where the police commonly use covert agents to infiltrate animal rights protests, environmental groups, and even public demonstrations against corporations. Some infiltrators spend years on their mission, living under fake identities,

cultivating purported friendships, and ultimately suc-
ceeding in spreading mistrust. The police file the names
and faces of protestors, and distributes that information
to private companies so they can avoid hiring them if they
ever apply for work.

The FBI also uses confidential informants in the so-called
War on Drugs. Some of those informants are convicted
criminals; others are thrown into crime by the FBI
itself. Statistics are hard to come by because the names
of informants are often kept secret, and the practice involves no mandatory paperwork. By some estimates, up
to eighty per cent of all drug investigations in the USA
entail the use of collaborators, and many of them, such
as Rachel Hoffman, do it under coercion. In 2008, the
23-year-old had just been accepted to a Master's program
in mental health counselling, through which she hoped
to get troubled kids to open up about their lives and
feelings while cooking together. Instead, she became CI
Hoffman, or Confidential Informant No. 1129, after police
found marijuana and ecstasy pills in her house. It was her
second offense—she had been previously stopped by the
police and found with an ounce of marijuana in her car.
Threatened with a jail sentence, Rachel was persuaded to
collaborate and spare her parents the shame of having a
daughter in prison.

Pressured by the police to reveal a drug dealer, Rachel
tried to set up a student she knew who dealt small quanti-
ties of drugs. But she regretted her betrayal, and went back
to confess and apologise, offering to pay his utility bills.
The student then tried to help her find someone that could

satisfy the Tallahassee police's demand for a big criminal, not a small-time pusher. Rachel finally got in touch with a major dealer and was instructed by the police to place an order that was so large it could only have brought suspicion upon her: 1,500 ecstasy pills, cocaine, and a handgun. Reassured by the police that nineteen of its men would wait in hiding to catch the dealer red-handed, she set up a meeting to close the deal. In short, the FBI sent Rachel, an untrained person, to meet a dangerous criminal that they knew would be armed. Wired and with an audio recorder in her purse, Rachel was still in touch with the police when the dealer asked her to drive to a new meeting place nearby. Her body was found days later, lying in a creek, shot five times with the very gun the police had sent her to buy.

There are several other tragic cases resulting from FBI blackmailing. LeBron Gaither, a 16-year-old student detained in Kentucky for punching a school assistant, was threatened with jail if he didn't become an FBI informant. Kept under coercion for years, Gaither was eighteen in 1996 when he was used in the sting operation that caught drug dealer Jason Noel. But the FBI also made Gaither testify in court against Noel, and after his release made Gaither meet Noel again. Gaither never left that meeting alive. His body was found after having been beaten, tortured, run over by a car and dragged in chains.

In 2011, 19-year-old Shelly Hilliard was caught smoking pot. Threatened with jail time, she accepted to help the FBI in the sting operation that caught drug dealer Qasim Raqib. But Raqib was released on the same day he was detained and hunted Hilliard down. Her body was found ablaze and dismembered afterwards, and Raqib confessed.

The GCHQ was established at the beginning of WWI to intercept and decipher military communication, and it has been credited with helping break the Enigma code. Today, it is the espionage agency in the UK tasked with the surveillance and collection of personal data of millions of people through monitoring their communications (emails, phones, website visits, text messaging, and written letters). Its mission is "to keep Britain safe and secure in the challenging environment of modern communications," or so the statement goes.

The GCHQ became better known to the public at large in July 2013, when its agents went to the newsroom of the London newspaper *The Guardian* and forced journalists to destroy computer hard disks that contained the Snowden files. With the help of an electric drill and angle-grinder, the destruction scene could have resembled scenes from *Fahrenheit 451*, but the final effect was more like that of a crazy person hitting an empty piñata, as all those documents were simultaneously in the possession of *The New York Times* and *The Washington Post*. The files—thousands of classified documents—revealed that the NSA and the GCHQ had been conducting a wide and indiscriminate surveillance of everyone. Even sexually explicit images from private Yahoo webcam chats were collected by GCHQ with the help of a program named Optic Nerve. The software, called Optic Perv by writer Graham Templeton, captured in a single six-month period in 2008 shots from 1.8 million Yahoo accounts.

The collaboration between the NSA and GCHQ goes way beyond the purview of the Five Eyes consortium. Through the documents leaked by Snowden, it was revealed that the NSA secretly paid around $150 million to its British counterpart for joint surveillance, an amount to which American taxpayers may object when they learn that the GCHQ gets the larger part of a budget that in 2013 alone was $ 2.9 billion.

The feared KGB was officially dissolved in 1991, but its remit stayed. The successors, FSB and SVR, are like two new IDs given by a handler to a veteran spy: new names, same old mission. While the FSB oversees counterterrorism, surveillance, and border control, the SVR is the foreign intelligence service handling Russia's interests abroad with the same tools used by its major counterparts: sabotage, assassination, and intelligence collection. The two agencies, however, share one unstated assignment: the persecution of political dissidents.

The list of adversaries of the Russian government who end up mysteriously dead in Britain is rather long, and the investigation into them by the UK intelligence services is meagre and patently flawed. One such assassination was that of former FSB official Alexander Litvinenko, who fled Russia after he became a whistle-blower against his employers. He died of polonium poisoning in London, days after meeting former colleagues for coffee. Though suspicion fell on the Russian government, no one has ever taken credit or accepted blame for the assassination, and it may be years before the facts are revealed.

There is one other criminal case in which the participation of the FSB is less ambiguous. Virtually unknown outside Russia, it changed the politics of that country in irreversible ways. In 1999, a series of four bombings at apartment buildings in Russia killed a total of almost 300 people. But, when the fifth terror attack in the same month was about to take place, something strange happened. On 22 September, residents of a building in the town of Ryazan noticed suspicious people unloading heavy sacks out of a car into the basement. Upon being spotted, the suspects took flight, leaving behind explosives, detonators, and a timer. The early detection thwarted a huge explosion. The next day, Vladimir Putin, recently appointed Prime Minister after having headed the FSB, blamed the attacks on Chechens and ordered the bombing of Grozny, the Chechen capital. Yet, despite Putin's stated certainty, the FSB in Ryazan was less convinced about the alleged culprits, and continued its investigation of the failed attack. By intercepting telephone calls, it surprisingly identified the involvement of FSB officers, people in their very midst. But to everyone's bigger shock, the government then suddenly changed its story and declared that the thwarted attack had actually been a simulation to test emergency response, and ordered the release of the suspects. Whether the government was saying the truth the first or the second time, Putin successfully turned Chechens into Public Enemy No. 1, much like it would happen to Arabs two years later with the 9/11 attacks. Shortly after, Putin ascended to the presidency, taking with him his experience as director of the FSB and his sixteen years as a KGB officer.

Russia is today at the vanguard of one of the most harmful intelligence missions: subversion, social disruption, sabotage, and a pervasive sense of mistrust. A groundbreaking story written by Adrian Chen for *The New York Times Magazine* exposed in the Latin alphabet what many people already knew in Cyrillic: that Russia fabricates disasters, creates chaos and manipulates public opinion in systematic ways through a factory of lies and false trends. The Internet Research Agency, as told by Chen, is a troll mill where hundreds of employees working twelve-hour shifts are paid roughly the same as local tenured professors to create fake social media accounts and feed each others' pages with false opinions, helping make all those accounts look popular and legitimate. Some of those fake accounts are used to boost Putin's image and to destroy that of his enemies. But there is another, more obscure, purpose to that factory.

Chen begun his research by investigating what started as an orchestrated panic about a chemical plant fire in the US State of Louisiana, a fire that never existed but still spread so wide and large through social media that it ended up scaring residents and grabbing the time and attention of national emergency offices. The hoax was disturbingly well-performed. It showed not only tweets and Facebook posts with the hashtag #ColumbianChemicals, but it included eyewitness accounts and even videos of the non-existent fire. The Russian troll factory also created panic about a false Ebola outbreak in America with significant attention to detail, including a video showing "hazmat-suited medical workers transporting a victim from the airport." In that clip, a Beyoncé song could be heard in the background, giving the images a subtle, legitimate-sounding time stamp.

The Internet Research Agency, owned by an ally of president Vladimir Putin, was also caught creating fake black movements in America, spreading false news about the police killing of an unarmed black woman in Atlanta, and arranging for personal defence classes for African-Americans through a group called Black Fist. The exact purpose of the Russian agency is not known, but its employees impersonate leftists and right-wing campaigners, antagonising real people on both sides and creating further dissension. Less than two years after this story was published in 2015, Russia was suspected of having influenced the US elections, accused of having 'paid for' ads for the election of Donald Trump, and believed to have hacked the Democratic National Convention.

CHAPTER EIGHT

OF PARASOLS AND PIGEONS

Of all the incredible espionage gadgets in films and spy novels, few are so absurdly improbable as the 'acoustic kitty'. The Acoustic Kitty Project was developed in the 1960s by the CIA, and according to former agent Victor Marchetti, it cost the government a whopping $20 million. The cat—a real one—had a microphone surgically implanted in its ear canal and a transmitter inserted at the base of its skull, the two connected by a wire under the cat's skin. Its first mission was to eavesdrop on men near the Soviet compound in Washington but, as soon as the cat was deployed, it was fatally hit by a taxi. The CIA disputes that story, saying the project was aborted even before its first mission because the agency had enormous difficulty in getting the cat to collaborate. It was only revealed in 2001, after an American citizen requested that the relevant documents be released under the Freedom of Information Act. A great instrument at the disposal of American citizens, the Freedom of Information Act (known as FOIA) can be easily exercised with the help of MuckRock, a non-profit organization that helps citizens get access to classified information.

Given the existence of an eavesdropping cat, it shouldn't come as a surprise that Egypt detained a stork for espionage in 2013. The purported spy was caught by a fisherman who noticed a suspicious item wrapped around its leg, later found to be a tracking device placed by scientists to monitor its migration. Animals have been used in espionage for centuries. Carrier pigeons were deployed in the sixth century BC by Cyrus II, King of Persia, and were used extensively during the two World Wars in Europe to carry messages and microfilms. Cher Ami, a female homing pigeon, was awarded her own Croix de Guerre by the French military for her work delivering messages at the Battle of Verdun. In 2001, the Director General of MI5, Stephen Lander, revealed that the counter-espionage agency had received help from Mossad to train gerbils to detect a rise in adrenaline levels as a way of spotting terrorists about to board planes. The disingenuous plan failed because non-terrorists boarding planes also frequently suffer from increased adrenaline levels due to good old fear of flying. The US Navy is home to the Marine Mammal Program, where it trains dolphins to identify underwater mines using echolocation, their biological sonar. It also teaches sea lions to retrieve objects. In Kuwait, US Marines used trained chickens to detect chemicals. In 2007, *Sky News* reported that the Iranian government burst a spy ring of fourteen squirrels it caught on the border wearing listening devices.

Inanimate objects are still, of course, the preferred tools in espionage. Gadgets are usually employed for three distinct purposes: surveillance, concealment, and assassination. The first includes cameras and microphones, which nowadays can fit inside almost anything: jacket buttons, sunglasses, purses, rings. Technology and mass production are making such products widely available and cheap, and made-in-China glasses fitted with concealed cameras can be bought for less than $20. Cameras and microphones can also be stationary and fitted inside teddy bears, television sets, lamps, paintings. Initially with their sale restricted to intelligence agencies, espionage tools are now in the hands of the public, and newspapers. One notorious case of illegal surveillance was perpetrated by the *News of the World*, a British newspaper belonging to Rupert Murdoch, investigated in 2005 for hacking the telephones of politicians, celebrities, the royal family, as well as crime victims and their relatives.

Perhaps the most iconic assassination gadget, along with the lipstick and the smoking pipe pistol, was an umbrella used against the Bulgarian writer and dissident Georgi Markov. In September 1978, Markov was in London walking to his office at the BBC when he felt a sharp pain on his thigh. He turned back to look, and saw a man pick an umbrella up from the ground, run across the street and get into a cab. Markov still went to work, but that night he fell down with a fever and went to the hospital, dying four days later from poisoning. The murder is thought to have been carried out by the KGB on behalf of the communist Bulgarian government. While the culprits' names have never been confirmed, the method used to kill Markov has been thoroughly examined. During the autopsy of his body, pathologists found a metal pellet the size of a pinhead with two tiny holes in it. Inside the pellet were traces of the deadly poison ricin, and the pellet holes had been sealed with a material set to melt at 36.6 °C, the human body's temperature.

Should all espionage gadgets fail, spies and soldiers alike can make use of another invention, the suicide pill. Developed by American and British intelligence during WWII, the cyanide pill was to be taken if painful death was imminent or, closer to its original spirit, if a soldier or agent risked revealing strategic secrets under torture. In 1960, a CIA U-2 spy plane was shot down while flying over Soviet airspace, but pilot Francis Gary Powers failed to take his assigned poison hidden in a tiny needle inside a hollow coin. After two years in Soviet captivity he was finally exchanged for another prisoner, yet Powers didn't return home as a hero. He was criticised for failing to activate the plane's self-destruct mechanism, and then failing to take his suicide contraption, the only two ways of ensuring his secrets remained private.

One contrivance you probably won't see in a *007* movie is the sick pill: aimed mostly at the faint of heart, its main purpose is to save secret agents from having to join an assignment in which they don't want to take part. As soon as the pill is ingested, it prompts sudden, uncontrollable vomiting, rendering the person incapacitated.

One contrivance you probably won't see in a 007 movie is the sick pill: aimed mostly at the faint of heart, its main purpose is to save secret agents from having to join an assignment in which they don't want to take part.

From WWI until after WWII, one of the most widely-used contraptions in espionage was the German-engineered Enigma, a typewriter-like machine used to encrypt messages. A paradigm shift at the time, the Enigma generated millions of possible combinations for each letter, making decryption almost impossible without the key tables codifying each letter. The machine is blamed with helping General Franco win the Spanish Civil War, but also credited to have aided the Allied Forces in defeating Germany once its codes were cracked.

Currently, the tool most widely touted for safe, encrypted Internet navigation is TOR. Partly made possible by DARPA, an agency of the US Department of Defence, and developed by the US Naval Research Laboratory, TOR stands for The Onion Router, a network through which information is encrypted and forwarded through thousands of relays, or nodes, making it presumably untraceable. Originally created to maintain the anonymity of government agents, it's only useful to intelligence agencies if regular people use it. The logic is simple: if only government agents use a network, anything done within that network can be traced back to the government. But TOR may have fatal flaws. Exit nodes—the final step through which the information in TOR is relayed—can be run by anyone, including the CIA. Data leakage has been reported, but some experts contest those charges. TOR is "the king of high-secure, low-latency Internet anonymity" and has "no contenders for the throne in waiting," two very encouraging statements if you don't mind the fact that they were said by the NSA itself, in a purportedly leaked "top-secret" document.

Before technology, ingenuity was key to protecting secret communications. In 1942, the US army recruited about 200 Navajo natives to help in the war efforts as code talkers, because their language was naturally 'encrypted': it was exclusively oral, and its grammar was virtually unknown outside the reservation. Another important tool was invisible ink: a dye that disappears once it is used in writing, only to reappear later with the help of a reacting agent. In his diary, British general Walter Kirke claims to have heard from Mansfield Smith-Cumming, the first director of the MI6, that the best invisible ink—to say nothing of its abundant availability—was human semen.

CHAPTER NINE

THE NEW AGE OF ESPIONAGE

Only a week after the 9/11 attacks, President George W. Bush told people at a press conference, "Through my tears, I see opportunity." Seven months later, Secretary of State Condoleezza Rice echoed a similar sentiment, repeating the word for the hard of hearing: "This is a period not just of grave danger, but of enormous opportunity. Before the clay is dry again, America and our friends and our allies must move decisively to take advantage of these new opportunities." And advantage they took.

Dick Cheney, Defence Secretary under Bush Sr and Vice President under Bush Jr who was also the CEO of Halliburton in between those two government posts, held tightly to his shares in the company as the US invaded Iraq, wasting $2 trillion of taxpayer money on the wrong target, and killing more than 100,000 civilians in the process, whilst giving Halliburton $6 billion in defence contracts and another $18 billion in oil-related deals.

On the national front of the so-called War on Terror, the government avoided missing the target by targeting everyone, spying on Americans at a never-before-seen scale, and creating a surveillance state that some experts compare to East Germany under the Stasi. Indeed, the government didn't wait for the clay to dry, and a mere nine days after the attacks, the US Congress authorised the executive to take an extra $40 billion to fight Al Qaeda. Since then, the US intelligence budget has multiplied every year, reaching $80 billion in 2010—a figure that doesn't include several domestic counterterrorism and military programs.

An award-winning, two-year-long investigation conducted by *The Washington Post* concluded, "The top-secret world the government created in response to the terrorist attacks of Sept. 11, 2001, has become so large, so unwieldy and so secretive that no one knows how much money it costs, how many people it employs, how many programs exist within it or exactly how many agencies do the same work." Worse yet, it is impossible to determine whether this is making the US any safer.

Retired army Lt. Gen. John R. Vines was tasked with reviewing the most sensitive programs conducted by the Defence Department. His conclusion was that the system is so absurdly complex that it is impossible to "effectively assess whether it is making us more safe." The title of the *Post*'s investigation summarizes its findings: "A Hidden World, Growing Beyond Control". And it shows no sign of abating. In September 2017, the Trump administration quietly renewed for the sixteenth time the state of emergency.

Commonly used by dictatorships and countries at war, the declaration of a state of emergency gives a president extraordinary powers, allowing them to circumvent the law to seize property, summon a national militia, cancel habeas corpus, and hire and fire military officers at will. As the powers of the government increase, the rights of citizens diminish. During a state of emergency there's much wider latitude to what the government can qualify as treason. Such unchecked power allowed the Obama administration to persecute more whistle-blowers than any other US presidency, most of them under the Espionage Act—the very same 1917 law used to condemn real traitors who spied on the US for Russia, like Robert Hanssen and Aldrich Ames. One of those whistle-blowers was William Binney.

For thirty-two years, Binney was a top mathematician and cryptanalyst at the NSA. He had always agreed with the agency's core mission of targeted surveillance on potential foreign terrorists, but resigned after realizing that the stated purpose had been subverted. In 2007, police raided his house and arrested him at gunpoint as he was taking a shower. Binney was suspected of leaking details of Stellar Wind, an NSA program that entailed broad and arbitrary spying of Americans, including the surveillance of their financial transactions and phone conversations. Stellar Wind "was highly classified only because it was domestic spying," Binney explains, so the government could keep secret "the extreme, impeachable crimes they were committing." Even FBI agents seemed to agree that Stellar Wind was inefficient, and that it cast a net so wide and

A dystopian, yet under-examined facet of intelligence privatisation: while taxpayers are prevented from knowing what is happening, investors and business partners are given privileged access.

illogical that new leads were referred to as 'pizza cases', since many of them proved to be just take-away food orders. But what may have really spelled Binney's troubles was his criticism of the NSA's privatisation of domestic espionage with Trailblazer, an ineffective (and later recalled) $280-million program led by a consortium that included private behemoths Booz Allen and Boeing.

According to the *Washington Post* report, while there are about 1,271 government organisations working in homeland security, intelligence and counterterrorism, the number of private companies contracted for the same job is fifty per cent bigger, at 1,931. In his book *Spies for Hire*, journalist Tim Shorrock reveals that seventy per cent of the US intelligence budget is spent on private sector contracts. Shorrock's own research illustrates the dangers of such a situation, as he got most of the material for his book—information that could theoretically jeopardise US security—by attending investor conferences and reading up on documents filed to the Securities and Exchange Commission. That illustrates a dystopian, yet under-examined facet of intelligence privatisation: while taxpayers are prevented from knowing what is happening, investors and business partners are given privileged access. "I think it's foolish of the intelligence agencies to accuse us [journalists] of somehow compromising national security. If you want to keep the stuff secret, don't contract it out to private companies who sell their stocks on the stock market," Shorrock says. He notes an even bigger problem: how can the government rely on threat assessments made by a company that profits from that very threat in the first place, and which obviously wants to renew its contracts?

"Do you think they're going to downplay the threat? Do you think they're going to say, 'Oh, there's no more problem over here in this area of the world, so we can just pull our contract'?"

There is a reason why enlightened governments keep firefighting as a public responsibility from which no one profits: because anyone rewarded to extinguish a fire also has the incentive to start it. That's what happened in Constantinople with the Tulumbadschi, the firefighting squads culpable for much of the blaze they were paid to put out. It's a reality that follows an overwhelming logic, a Newton's Law of Duh describing an inescapable sequence: start paying a handsome reward for the elimination of man-made tragedies, and those tragedies will invariably grow.

In an ideal world, espionage would serve to prevent wars and reduce casualties in conflicts already started. Brains would replace force, sparing lives and avoiding destruction. In *Shadow Knights*, Gary Kamiya tells the WWII story of two teenage girls who, working as agents for the French, rode their bicycles to where the German trains were hidden and sabotaged them, replacing the axle oil with abrasive grease and, in doing so, prevented some of the Wehrmacht's Panzer tanks from arriving at the Normandy beachhead before D-Day. Disinformation was another tool successfully used by the Allied forces before the invasion of Sicily. In Operation Mincemeat, British intelligence released from a submarine off the coast of Spain a corpse dressed in a Royal Marine uniform with secret papers concerning an Allied invasion of Greece. German intelligence swallowed the ruse, and Hitler diverted significant resources from Sicily and Russia to Greece.

In our times, however, war and espionage have become symbiotic industries justifying each other's existence, the fireman and the fire working seamlessly for the perpetual motion of this wheel of fortune where espionage produces excuses for war, and the fear of war produces the need for more espionage.

It stands to reason that an umbrella salesman hopes for bad weather, but while he profits from the rain he cannot summon it. Counterterrorists, however, can create terror—indeed they have all the necessary weapons and advantages that criminals could only dream of: guaranteed anonymity, guns and funds, illegal and untraceable money, government connections and cover-ups, oversight, immunity, and a pervasive lack of constraint. The privatisation of war and espionage is immoral, first and foremost, because it provides the industry with all the means to create its own necessity, and it is thus inefficient by design. It is mind-boggling that citizens agree so eagerly to fund a business that will only thrive if things get worse. Without public scrutiny, restraint, or punishment on one hand, and with a financial reward that increases as its target grows on the other, the ever-widening hammer of the War on Something goes unabated, expanding its own nail.

More worryingly yet, the revolving doors between government and industry further taint the pursuit of the common good with the interference of private interests. Michael Chertoff, former Homeland Security Chief in the governments of George W. Bush and Barack Obama, who had knowledge of classified government information and could get access to virtually anyone's phone or email, left the government to head a company that sells security consultancy to the government. His business partner is Michael Hayden, former Director of the National Security Agency. Another company contracted by the government is IronNet Cybersecurity—owned by Keith Alexander, the longest-serving director in the history of the NSA who was once trusted with the highest security clearance in the country.

Because the actual motivation for war is often money, war merchants need the fabrication of lofty motives to persuade the public to bankroll these incredibly costly and, for them, incredibly profitable ventures. Espionage agencies have been crucial in the production of those narratives, inventing realities through their departments of black ops and clandestine operations, causing dissent, creating false enemies, spreading mistrust and, perhaps more noxiously, rendering reality almost ungraspable to the average people consuming the news made by companies controlled by weapons merchants. And here lies much of the disconnect between pacifists and warmongers: critics of wars ignore that supporters of wars are ignorant.

With the exception of those directly benefiting from the most lucrative enterprise known to man, there is no inherent evil in supporting a war if one believes that war is a great tragedy preventing a bigger one. More often than not, the person defending a war is just another victim of the same farce. People who are at once intelligent, well-informed and honest generally agree that it would be better for most of the world if the trillions spent on war and defence were invested on things that make people want to

Espionage agencies have been inventing realities through their departments of black ops and clandestine operations, causing dissent, creating false enemies, spreading mistrust and, perhaps more noxiously, rendering reality almost ungraspable to the average people consuming the news made by companies controlled by weapons merchants.

live, rather than die: culture, knowledge, beauty, nature, peace, art, far niente. This would also make for a much safer world. The most dangerous men are the ones who have nothing to lose, and wars are excellent at creating them. Wars also create perpetual resentment, inoculating people with a persistent bad blood that takes generations to dissolve. This mistrust is also spread by espionage, often unintentionally.

Of all the espionage agencies, Mossad is usually seen as the most legitimate, with a purported mandate that many consider genuine—that of protecting Jews worldwide. Even enemies of Israel and opponents of its illegal occupation know that throughout the ages Jews have been the indisputable victims of hatred and persecution. How is it reasonable, then, that Mossad itself helps sow further suspicion of the Jews by tapping them in search of sayanim, Zionists willing to work as ad hoc agents ready to lie and spy under the inviolable orders of God and nation? How is it acceptable that the same agency claiming to exist for the protection of the Jews makes them all impending targets of fear and distrust by rounding them all as a group from which they may get secret collaborators? And what happens to the countless Jews who refuse to join? Are they considered traitors? Lesser Jews?

In *The Devil's Chessboard*, David Talbot makes it clear that behind the CIA's inception, and for a good while at its helm, was a man, Allen Dulles, whose main mandate was to work for Wall Street and the world's leading plutocrats. For that, he and the CIA followed directives given even before the agency's beginning by William J. Donovan, the head of the CIA's precursor, OSS. In a hand-signed manual published by MuckRock, Donovan delineates the 'basic doctrine' of the CIA's predecessor for psy-ops. They include, verbatim: manipulation of individuals and underground groups; agents provocateurs; bribery and blackmail; rumours; forgery; false leaflets. It also recommends that agents drug their targets so that they can be blackmailed later for having used drugs. There were bound to be occasions "when incriminating information is difficult to secure, or when no such information exists." In these instances, "it may be possible either to create or to plant it."

Of course there are good spies, and whistle-blowers are there to prove it. One of them, US Army intelligence officer Christopher Pyle, made revelations of illegal military espionage of civilians that resulted in the 1975 Church Committee, an unprecedented, hair-raising US senate investigation of intelligence activities. Little has changed since, but the committee has at least served to give weight to two long-scorned truisms: "A conspiracy theorist may just be someone who knows more than you do," and, as US Army general Dwight Eisenhower warned when stepping down from the US presidency, later even more succinctly put by Frank Zappa: "Politics is the entertainment division of the military-industrial complex."

AFTERWORD

OF MICE AND RATS

The goal of this book was to make some sense of the underground world of intelligence, and to do so concisely—I agreed to that condition. As an editor in Cairo, I abolished from our newsroom the widespread incongruence of paying writers per word. More words do not equal more information, and the media coverage of espionage is evidence of that. Raise your hand if, through all the news about the War on Terror, you learned that since 9/11 the FBI has manufactured more terror plots on US soil than any other group or individual. You probably didn't know either that the US government was behind the death of as many as 10,000 Americans who drank liquor spiked with poison during the Prohibition era. These are not just morbid nuggets—they are factual precedents that should inform every reading of official narratives.

When it comes to concision, the shorter the book, the longer is the time spent on identifying the essential. I hope I managed to do some of it here. I urge the reader, however, to go deeper, and use this as a guide to further research. For those who can't afford the time, I trust that this book will help give them a less naïve view of the invisible power that rules over us with minimum or no oversight. If I did in part succeed, much of the credit must go to the painstaking work of investigation carried out by the authors of the articles and books quoted here, and to people I interviewed, most of them anonymously.

This book was also informed by personal experience. Although I cannot claim to have first-hand knowledge of spying, in all these years as a political journalist, and more so in my decade as a Middle East correspondent, I interviewed with exclusivity several targets of international espionage and attempted assassinations, specifically: Hassan Nasrallah, the Secretary General of the Shia group Hezbollah; Saad Hariri, the Lebanese Prime Minister; Fernando Gabeira, one of the kidnappers of the US ambassador to Brazil Charles Elbrick; Leila Khaled, the Palestinian revolutionary and first woman to successfully hijack a plane; Salman Rushdie, during the time when the writer was still under Scotland Yard protection from an Iranian death sentence and had a $3 million bounty on his head. I also interviewed at least one person who was almost certainly at the other end of assassination attempts, Shabtai Shavit, head of Mossad from 1989 to 1996.

If my experience in the espionage field is poor, it has still gone beyond what I had wished. Years after meeting Hassan Nasrallah, I was detained by Hezbollah agents on suspicion of espionage after they saw me taking photos in a Shia area for my Master's thesis at the American University of Beirut. They took my driver and me to a building, and locked each of us in a numbered room used for interrogation—a mistake they corrected soon after with apologies, coffee and cookies (this story was eventually told in the Brazilian edition of *Rolling Stone*).

I hope that this book will entice the reader to enquire further into the most important, yet widely ignored, aspect of espionage and wars: the goals, as opposed to the means. Even good journalists prefer to spend pages discussing methods euphemised as 'extraordinary rendition' and 'enhanced interrogation', focusing on the means rather than examining the legitimacy of those ends, and thus unwittingly doing the bidding of the intelligence outfits. Espionage agencies want us to keep debating the means, because that is precisely where the debate becomes never-ending, as there will always be people who think the end justifies them. It is the end, therefore, that we should be probing. Does government-mandated espionage make for a safer country? Is it being used for the public good or for private interests? And, is espionage an effect that is perhaps concocting its own cause?

Endless debate on the means is a favourite 'limited hangout': a ruse by which intelligence agencies promote, leak, or even confess to negative stories about themselves so as to avoid investigation into yet unknown but more damaging facts. The revelation of the Iran-Contra affairs—when the US illegally sold weapons to an enemy country so as to fund and arm right-wing militias fighting against a socialist government—is thought by many serious investigators to be a limited hangout. I am one of those who believe there is a much darker, criminal and immoral story beneath that account, one that lacks the camouflage of ideology or patriotism.

The most disturbing truth about the espionage industry is that, much like what US president Eisenhower called 'the military industrial complex', it hardly ever works for the nations it purports to represent. It works instead for corporations and their shareholders in a big swindle where the taxpayer not only accepts, but indeed demands to sponsor such unverifiable work. In 2016 alone, US taxpayers spent $70.7 billion on intelligence. The military budget was over half a trillion dollars. In 2017, under the presidency of Donald Trump, with Capitol Hill as divided as it has ever been, Republicans and Democrats united in the Senate voting 89-9 to give the Pentagon $700 billion of taxpayers' money, $28 billion above what Trump had originally asked for.

Decades ago, Smedley Butler, the retired general who died as the most decorated Marine in US history, declared to have discovered far too late that all the wars he fought for his country were rackets for private interests:

> I helped make Mexico and especially Tampico safe for American oil interests in 1914. I helped make Haiti and Cuba a decent place for the National City Bank boys to collect revenues in. I helped in the raping of half a dozen Central American republics for the benefit of Wall Street. I helped purify Nicaragua for the International Banking House of Brown Brothers in 1902-1912. I brought light to the Dominican Republic for the American sugar interests

in 1916. I helped make Honduras right for the American fruit companies in 1903. In China in 1927 I helped see to it that Standard Oil went on its way unmolested.

Today, Butler and his message have been all but wiped from history textbooks. Instead, corporations and their media and entertainment associates have rewritten reality, working in unison to cement in the collective psyche the association between corporations and country, nationalism and violent protectionism. That is why the US Department of Defence gives millions of taxpayer's money to NASCAR, NFL and other major-league sports to have them perform military propaganda at their games. Companies need that people see them as truly American, or Russian, or Brazilian, even if they hardly ever benefit the citizens or the soil on which they stand. Their national aspect serves mostly as a jersey identifying a team on a manufactured field of dissent, where players fight but the puppet masters never lose, all while the one cheering from the sofa is funding the show and getting nothing in return but fleeting entertainment and a false sense of purpose.

"Since agencies control the news they release, and ensure its uncritical dissemination through their own people in the media world, all spy stories should be treated with extreme scepticism."

—Phillip Knightley
The Second Oldest Profession

BIBLIOGRAPHY & FURTHER READINGS

Aaronson, Trevor. 2013. *The Terror Factory: Inside the FBI's Manufactured War on Terrorism*. Brooklyn, New York: Ig Publishing.

Abrahamian, Ervand. 2013. *The Coup: 1953, The CIA, and The Roots of Modern U.S.-Iranian Relations*. New York: The New Press.

Ben-Menashe, Ari. 1992. *Profits of War: Inside the Secret U.S.-Israeli Arms Network*. New York: Sheridan Square Press.

Cialdini, Robert B. 2008. *Influence: Science and Practice*. Boston: Pearson.

Cockburn, Andrew, and Leslie Cockburn. 1991. *Dangerous Liaison: The Inside Story of the U.S.-Israeli Covert Relationship*. New York: HarperCollins.

Cohen, Jacob. 2010. *Le Printemps des Sayanim*. Paris: Harmattan.

Dunlop, John B. 2012. *The Moscow Bombings of September 1999: Examinations of Russian Terrorist Attacks at the Onset of Vladimir Putin's Rule*. Stuttgart: Ibidem-Verlag.

Feinstein, Andrew. 2012. *The Shadow World: Inside the*

Global Arms Trade. New York: Picador Farrar, Straus and Giroux.

Harding, Luke. 2014. *The Snowden Files: The Inside Story of the World's Most Wanted Man*. London: Guardian Faber Publishing.

Hersh, Seymour M. 1991. *The Samson Option: Israel's Nuclear Arsenal and American Foreign Policy*. New York: Random House.

Jeffery, Keith. 2011. *The Secret History of MI6*. New York: Penguin Books.

Kamiya, Gary. 2010. *Shadow Knights: The Secret War Against Hitler*. New York: Simon & Schuster.

Kinzer, Stephen. 2008. *All the Shah's Men: An American Coup and the Roots of Middle East Terror*. Hoboken: John Wiley & Sons.

Knightley, Phillip. 1986. *The Second Oldest Profession: The Spy as Bureaucrat, Patriot, Fantasist and Whore*. London: André Deutsch.

Knightley, Phillip. 2004. *The First Casualty: The War Correspondent as Hero and Myth-Maker from the Crimea to Iraq*. Baltimore: Johns Hopkins University Press.

Ostrovsky, Victor, and Claire Hoy. 1990. *By Way of Deception*. New York: St. Martin's Press.

Perkins, John. 2006. *Confessions of an Economic Hit Man*. New York: Plume.

Philby, Kim. 2002. *My Silent War: The Autobiography of a*

Spy. New York: Modern Library.

Raviv, Dan, and Yossi Melman. 1990. *Every Spy a Prince: The Complete History of Israel's Intelligence Community*. Boston: Houghton Mifflin.

Scahill, Jeremy. 2007. Blackwater: *The Rise of the World's Most Powerful Mercenary Army*. New York: Nation Books.

Shorrock, Tim. 2008. Spies for Hire: *The Secret World Of Intelligence Outsourcing*. New York: Simon & Schuster.

Stockwell, John. 1984. *In Search Of Enemies: A CIA Story*. New York: Norton.

Talbot, David. 2016. *The Devil's Chessboard: Allen Dulles, the CIA, and the Rise of America's Secret Government*. New York: Harper Perennial.

Thomas, Gordon. 2000. *Gideon's Spies: The Secret History of the Mossad*. New York: St. Martin's Griffin.

Unger, Craig. 2004. *House of Bush, House of Saud: The Secret Relationship Between the World's Two Most Powerful Dynasties*. New York: Scribner.

U.S. Joint Chiefs of Staff. Justification for US Military Intervention in Cuba (TS). In U.S. Department of Defence, 13 March 1962. National Security Archive at the George Washington University Gelman Library, Washington, D.C. (https://nsarchive2.gwu.edu/news/20010430/northwoods.pdf, accessed 25 November 2017)

Wilford, Hugh. 2008. *The Mighty Wurlitzer: How the CIA Played America*. Cambridge: Harvard University Press.

CURIOUS READS ...are short books that connect the dots on topics that matter; topics everyone reads about, hears about, and talks about. Written by subject-matter experts for nonspecialist readers, they are accessible, concise, and beautifully produced.

ALSO OUT:

Vampires: Lovesick & Bloodthirsty
Justin E.H. Smith

Water Wars: Fight to the Last Drop
Frederika Whitehead

Immortality: Live Forever or Die Trying
Guy Weress

Privacy: How to Get it Back
BJ Mendelson

www.curiousreads.net